THE GLOBAL SPREAD
OF ARMS

DILEMMAS IN WORLD POLITICS

Series Editor
George A. Lopez, University of Notre Dame

Dilemmas in World Politics offers teachers and students of international relations a series of quality books on critical issues, trends, and regions in international politics. Each text examines a "real world" dilemma and is structured to cover the historical, theoretical, practical, and projected dimensions of its subject.

FORTHCOMING TITLES

Ted Robert Gurr and Barbara Harff
Ethnic Conflict in World Politics

□ □ □

Deborah J. Gerner
**One Land, Two Peoples:
The Conflict over Palestine, second edition**

□ □ □

Gareth Porter and Janet Welsh Brown
Global Environmental Politics, second edition

□ □ □

Bruce E. Moon
International Trade in the 1990s

□ □ □

Karen Mingst and Margaret P. Karns
The United Nations in the Post–Cold War Era

THE GLOBAL SPREAD OF ARMS

■ ■ ■

Political Economy of International Security

Frederic S. Pearson

WAYNE STATE UNIVERSITY

Westview Press

BOULDER □ SAN FRANCISCO □ OXFORD

For Beverly, Robert, and Rhonda
Eyes open to the world

Dilemmas in World Politics

Published in 1994 in the United States of America by Westview Press, Inc., 5500 Central Avenue, Boulder, Colorado 80301-2877, and in the United Kingdom by Westview Press, 36 Lonsdale Road, Summertown, Oxford OX2 7EW

Library of Congress Cataloging-in-Publication Data
Pearson, Frederic S.
  The global spread of arms : political economy of international security / Frederic S. Pearson.
    p.   cm. — (Dilemmas in world politics)
  Includes bibliographical references and index.
  ISBN 0-8133-1573-5. — ISBN 0-8133-1574-3 (pbk.)
  1. Arms race.   2. Arms transfers.   3. Defense industries—Social aspects.   4. Security, International.   I. Title.   II. Series.
UA10.P43   1994
327.1'74—dc20   94-8108
                                                                              CIP

Printed and bound in the United States of America

The paper used in this publication meets the requirements of the American National Standard for Permanence of Paper for Printed Library Materials Z39.48-1984.

10   9   8   7   6   5   4   3   2   1

Contents

□ □ □

Tables and Illustrations

Figures

Cartoons

Photos

□ □ □

Acknowledgments

I wish to thank my colleagues on the Westview Dilemmas series editorial board for their constructive advice, George Lopez for excellent feedback on ideas and resources, and especially Jennifer Knerr for her stalwart guidance and calm encouragement.

Special gratitude goes to my wife, Melvadean, who provided wise counsel and a crash computer graphics course to make this readable.

Frederic S. Pearson

□   □   □

Acronyms

ASAT	antisatellite
BAe	British Aerospace Corporation
CAT	Conventional Arms Transfer
CFE	Conventional Forces in Europe
CIA	Central Intelligence Agency
CIS	Commonwealth of Independent States
CWC	Chemical Weapons Convention
EC	European Community
FARC	Revolutionary Armed Forces of Colombia
FRG	Federal Republic of Germany
FSU	former Soviet Union
GNP	gross national product
GRIT	graduated and reciprocated initiative in tension-reduction
IAEA	International Atomic Energy Agency
IGO	intergovernmental organization
IISS	International Institute for Strategic Studies
IRA	Irish Republican Army
KGB	State Security Agency
LDC	less developed country
MAD	mutual assured destruction
MIRV	multiple independently targeted reentry vehicle
MTCR	Missile Technology Control Regime
NATO	North Atlantic Treaty Organization
NIC	newly industrializing country
NPT	Nuclear Non-proliferation Treaty
OAS	Organization of American States
OAU	Organization of African Unity
OECD	Organization for Economic Cooperation and Development
PLO	Palestine Liberation Organization
SALT	Strategic Arms Limitation Talks
SIPRI	Stockholm International Peace Research Institute
SOPS	standard operating procedures
START	Strategic Arms Reduction Treaty
TTBT	Threshold Test Ban Treaty

□   □   □

Introduction: Persistent
Arms Dilemmas

The end of the cold war between the United States and the USSR
seemed to usher in a moment of opportunity for peace in 1990. Major
power leaders in Washington and European capitals even began speaking
about the creation of global institutions to keep the peace and establish a
"new order," including controls on the spread of armament. Indeed, major powers in world politics share certain interests in controlling events in
various regions and preventing unwanted developments and actions.
When weapons become widely available to many governments and political groups (such as terrorists), attaining such control or order (often referred to as stability) is more difficult.

Although the cold war's end seemed to offer hope of a **peace dividend**
in limiting arms supplies and saving the cost of their production or purchase, it has since become clear that stemming the tide of global arms distribution is far more problematic than many suspected and that the major
powers themselves continue to play the pivotal role of weapons distributors. Despite **arms control** intentions (i.e., desires to limit the number or
types of weapons in countries' arsenals or available in international
trade), local wars continue to boil, and particular arms suppliers continue
to support their clients. Industrial manufacturers have established stakes
in weapons production; armed conflicts continued to attract arms shipments; and the demise of the Soviet bloc itself caused an added rush by
nearly destitute former communist states to sell more weapons abroad in
order to gain hard currency.

For centuries—certainly since the dawn of the nation-state system in
1648—armament has both fascinated and horrified the human mind. On
the one hand, weapons are seen as a means to greater security and freedom of action (autonomy) and a way of guarding hearth and home, especially when other forms of protection, such as the rule of law, are weak or
lacking. Major powers, which frequently rely on arms to enforce their will

1

on others, often fear that if others gain freer access to arms, they will resist more effectively and "destabilize" world politics. Weapons can thus diminish security and relative power by threatening opponents so that they arm in return, leading both sides to feel more vulnerable and more caught in a vicious armament spiral. The costs of such arms races mount in terms of resources expended and benefits foregone.

This question of uncertain security has been termed the *security dilemma* by those interested in studying international conflict. One can arm for security and influence but end up more insecure, "inheriting only the wind." The security dilemma is only one of several quandaries posed by the accumulation of weapons. These dilemmas, some of which are political and some of which are economic, are argued and debated in our everyday politics both at home and abroad.

The *dilemma of causation* is captured in the famous bumper sticker displayed by opponents of gun control in the United States: "Guns don't kill people; people kill people." This statement raises uncertainty about the effects of armament—does it constitute a sort of public health hazard that leads to more and more deaths? Skeptics argue that humans would find other ways to kill each other if firearms were eliminated; knives, poisons, or implements such as motor vehicles, for example, could be used to cause mayhem. However, others maintain that the availability of specialized weapons makes killing much easier—at the push of a button or pull of a trigger, so to speak—and therefore more prevalent than if people were forced to use other means. Certainly murder rates are higher in American cities where guns are readily available than in Canadian cities where they are effectively banned; but is this fact, as opposed to poverty levels, social conflicts, or other pressures, what leads to or *causes* violence?

The *dilemma of access* entails uncertainty about the effect of trying to eliminate arms. As with other prohibitions (notably alcoholic beverages in the United States during the 1920s or narcotic drugs more recently), it is argued that those most interested in obtaining the banned items would still find a way to do so and that illicit businesses would grow up to supply these consumers. The most violent would still find a way to obtain weapons, through contraband or black markets if necessary: "If guns are outlawed, only the outlaws will have guns." Some advocates of a "right to bear arms" argue that governing authorities cannot necessarily be trusted to own a monopoly of force in society and that citizens must be able to resist or make up for repressive or corrupt rulers. However, Western precepts regarding the rule of law also say that citizen vigilantes are dangerous and that well-trained professional police or soldiers provide a more rational and safer form of order. A dilemma exists, then, because those interested in peace ostensibly have to fight for it on occasion and because entitlement to be armed must be determined. This dilemma extends to international relations in questions about the wisdom of arming or forcefully disarming a Saddam Hussein or Somali "warlords" and of building a U.N. or **multilateral** (joint international) police force able to assure individual states and citizens of their rights and security.

The *dilemma of alternatives* means that finding alternatives to armament to promote security or trade (imports or exports) can be difficult, a mainly economic dilemma facing those interested in disarmament or peace. Upon assuming office in 1989, the humanistic Czech president Vaclav Havel promised to eliminate Czechoslovakia's checkered history of global arms sales, a legacy of the communist era. Yet he soon determined that to do so would dismantle one of the Slovak region's last viable industries, leading to economic ruin and therefore to national disintegration (Slovakian nationalists would rise up and call for independence). The lesser of two evils would be to continue selling guns and tanks to foreign markets, even at the risk of fueling wars. Ironically, however, even with continued arms sales, Czechoslovakia broke apart as a state in 1992 into the Czech Republic and Slovakia, both of which continued trying to sell arms.

U.S. politicians have used similar arguments in slowing the pace of a post–cold war peace dividend, maintaining defense spending in districts threatened with defense job losses. The easy rationalization is that "if the United States doesn't sell arms, someone else will." Some argue that such short-term solutions lead to long-term economic ruin, however; in 1993, citing recent studies, U.S. president Bill Clinton maintained that switching away from military production and closing military bases would provide greater economic benefits than military spending itself. However, at the same time Clinton's commerce secretary, Ron Brown, visited Europe to promote American weapons exports to North Atlantic Treaty Organization (NATO) allies.

The *adequacy dilemma* comprises the question, How much armament is enough? and is essentially a part of the security dilemma mentioned earlier. How well armed must a nation be to feel secure against attack by its neighbors, and is that a reasonable and limited or an open-ended and arbitrary level? Who would legitimately determine these answers, and by what procedure or criteria would they do so? Theoretically, in a system of sovereign independent states, governments decide for themselves how much is enough. But their decisions can play havoc with neighbors' security and regional balances of power. Should international authorities be established to determine both whose record is good enough to merit armament and at what level? One state, such as Israel or India, might feel obliged to arm against several neighbors at once (Syria, Iraq, and Iran for Israel; Pakistan and China for India). This would, in turn, lead each neighbor to respond in kind, with the result being a multiplier effect on regional armament (this type of pattern happened during the 1960s in the Middle East).[1]

The *political dilemma* requires that we recognize that the question of armament in international relations is not related simply to security or economic objectives. Politics becomes part of the debate as well since arms are a means to political power. Some leaders in fact shoot their way into office or depend on armed force to stay there. National governments sometimes seek to expand their foreign influence through the application of force. Therefore, even if all the other ingredients for arms reduction are in place, there is still the potential, and for some the irresistible temptation, to use arms to bolster political power. China's noted revolutionary strategist Mao Zedong was often quoted as saying that "power comes from the barrel of a gun."

The question, then, is whether or not to arm, under what authority, to what extent, and at what cost. Not every nation is intent upon or can afford to acquire extensive military arsenals. Nearly every independent nation-state, however, whether run by democratic or by authoritarian regimes, whether able to afford massive military spending or not, asserts the same sovereign right to arm. Here the dilemma of access becomes an *equity dilemma.* Should all states be allowed to develop and acquire new weapons? Or should only the six or seven nuclear-armed states or great powers be trusted with weapons of mass destruction? And are their leaders any more enlightened or trustworthy than those of smaller, poorer states? Is there a "double standard" about which states' arms developments are encouraged or tolerated and which are criticized and opposed?

In this volume, I touch upon the implications of all these dilemmas and raise an additional question in the wake of the twentieth century's disastrous and repetitive wars: Can the **proliferation,** or spread, of weapons around the globe be stopped? After the 1991 Gulf War, we saw a world organization, the United Nations, empowered to intervene, investigate, and judge the acceptability of a supposedly sovereign state's military arsenal. Subsequent disagreements over the extent of U.N. investigative authority and ability to find all weapons components in Iraq threatened to lead to renewed warfare. I ask whether this situation was a quirk or a developing international trend, as similar concerns and alarms were raised subsequently about suspected North Korean nuclear arms programs.

Weapons proliferation is a problem that has caught public attention in the past on the nuclear question; the fear of nuclear weapons spreading led to the **Nuclear Non-proliferation Treaty (NPT)** of 1968. Recently, with scenes of carnage in places such as the former Yugoslavia, Afghanistan, Northern Ireland, Cambodia, southern Africa, Liberia, Somalia, Sudan, Zaire, Haiti, Central America, Indonesia, and the Persian Gulf, concern has also been raised about easy access to conventional arms. Leaders

The complications of on-site weapons inspection: The Iraqi experience. Kirk/The Toledo Blade, OH/Rothco.

worry that many more countries will obtain not just tanks and jets but also weapons of mass destruction or high technology as well as the sophisticated means to deliver them against other countries. Whether this is an acute or an exaggerated worry and whether anything can or should be done about it are among the chief concerns discussed in this volume.

It is necessary to determine how and why the international trade and exchange of arms take place, including the history both of arms developments and arms limitation efforts. I review the policy and ethical dilemmas of trying to find alternatives to armament and ask which of the dilemmas of armament in world politics can be solved. The next chapter deals with both the history of arms proliferation and the latest global trends.

ONE

□ □ □

Global Arms Proliferation: Past and Present

The importance of weaponry in international relations goes far back in time. Strategically timed arms shipments, or transfers, for example, were used in ancient as well as modern times to fortify friends or weaken enemies, thus leading to the rise of political power and affecting the outcome of wars. Such policies can be traced at least as far back as the Peloponnesian Wars of the Greek city-states.[1] Although the effort to control others by providing them with weapons, or even by fighting them, does not always work, arms and armed forces do get leaders' attention. As Soviet leader Joseph Stalin was supposed to have said in reply to a question about whether he would heed the opinion of the pope, "How many divisions does the pope have?"

Arms transfers are defined here as the shipment of arms or related goods and services by sale, loan, or gift from one country to another; such shipments may be by one government to another, by a government to specific individuals or forces (e.g., rebels) abroad, or by a manufacturer to either a foreign government or forces. "Related goods and services" means such things as military base construction and logistical equipment for storing, launching, or servicing arms, which are sometimes included in arms trade deals. Ancient arms shipments probably had relatively few of these items built in, but for today's arms exporters, such as the United States or Britain, these add-ons can constitute a sizable share of the value of transfers.

Another tricky issue, therefore, is determining what constitutes arms. Clearly anything that can be used to inflict pain and suffering on an enemy is in a sense a weapon. In ancient times this would have included the wooden Trojan horse used to secrete soldiers into the enemy's home city; in modern times the pickup trucks the Palestine Liberation Organization (PLO) used to mount anti-aircraft guns against Israeli planes would

7

amount to much the same thing. Knowing what to count as a weapon of course affects efforts to limit their spread, as seen later in the book.

The world became **militarized** in the modern sense with the invention of the cannon in the fourteenth century and the subsequent age of military rivalry and production that it spawned.[2] Until then, little human attention had been focused on gaining advantages over opponents by improving weapons. Indeed, most of the forms of weaponry we are familiar with today had been invented and used by 600 B.C.—including varieties of armor, mobile forces (chariots or cavalry), missiles (thrown weapons), infantry weapons (originally clubs, spears, and axes), and fortified boats. They had been developed along with other implements with the dawn of the "Age of Tools" and metalworking, probably as offshoots of hunting or as protection from predators.[3] Certainly there had been key innovations, as in Roman adaptations of chariots, the Carthaginian use of elephants in the mountains, or the Spartan form of chemical warfare achieved by burning wood treated with sulphur and pitch to engulf enemies with clouds of sulphur dioxide.[4] Generally, however, warriors were satisfied with relatively predictable and similar weapons on both sides of battles.

Among so-called primitive tribes in remote parts of the tropics, for example, traditional warfare normally involved stylized ritualistic combat—groups of ceremonially decorated warriors danced, shouted, and confronted each other across a broad open battlefield or engaged in village raids, throwing spears, shooting arrows, or wielding axes. Engagements often broke off when a single enemy warrior was killed to assuage ancestors, ghosts, or gods or to clear the way for one group to expand its domain or grow more crops. No great effort was made to perfect new or better weapons to overwhelm the bows and arrows.[5]

Although there are some similarities here to modern warfare, how different such scenes look from the modern meeting of phalanxes of forces equipped with the latest weaponry and seeking mass destruction of the enemy or from even modern guerrilla war, with mobile forces attacking from hidden positions and using quick hit-and-run tactics. Apart from larger and more organized or professional armies fighting for supposedly grander political causes, one major difference is that with the dawn of the industrial age, specialists went to work devising ways to upgrade and improve arms, seeking major advantage over opponents through new technology in such fields as chemistry and metallurgy, an offshoot of the general tendency to support new inventions and discoveries. A special class of weapons designers and engineers emerged, even taking up some of the greatest artistic and scientific minds of history—including the likes of Michelangelo, Leonardo da Vinci, and the Soviet and U.S. physicists Andrei Sakharov and Robert Oppenheimer, respectively. The state, as it developed a reliable tax base, patronized and supported such technologists, a pattern that we see repeated today with some of the world's largest corporations. In general, then, weapons have tended to reflect the level of technological achievement and aspiration of the times.

But not all weapons innovations relate to uses in war. The motives for improving arms often have less to do with warfare itself than with technical, political, and economic factors.[6] Leaders desire new weapons for political purposes, such as conquest or influence with friends or foes; firms manufacture them for profit; both come to agree that power depends on new military technology.

Arms, then, are treated as symbols of power and glory in addition to being valued for use in battle. That is why, for example, weapons, both singly and collectively, always have been aesthetically decorated and even named by their owners or opponents: for example, the "Big Bertha" (named after the wife of its German manufacturer) artillery of World War I and the U.S. and British bombers, missiles, and warships of the post–World War II period. Some arms are designed to be used, some to be displayed—often the bigger the better. Before the Soviets were able to hit the United States with reliable intercontinental missiles, they paraded their biggest rockets through Red Square every May 1, in part to impress and frighten and perhaps even deceive the enemy and in part to inspire their own population. Leaders of the Ottoman Empire in Turkey invented the military parade band centuries ago for use in battle in part to do the same thing.

Nuclear weapons, although designed originally for battle, have gradually picked up a reputation for being too terrible to use. They join other weapons in history, notably the crossbow, red hot cannonballs, balloon-borne bombs, and dumdum (expanding) bullets, as being considered inhumane. A recent similar effort was mounted to ban various forms of land mines. But such designations have not entirely prevented the exchange or use of some of these feared devices. Humans are capable of employing truly grisly implements for motives of revenge or dominance, as when early American colonists traded smallpox-contaminated blankets to Indian tribes during the French and Indian Wars.[7] What may seem inhumane to some, however, can appear as legitimate defense to others; in Russia and Eastern Europe, princely armies used land spikes from the fifteenth through the seventeenth centuries to disable each other's horses. These techniques were later refined in explosive land mines and the bamboo spikes used by Vietnamese guerrillas against U.S. forces in the twentieth century. President Harry Truman claimed that his use of atomic bombs against the Japanese in World War II actually saved lives by hastening the end of the war. It appears easier to employ destructive weapons when the enemy is viewed as ruthless, inhumane, and aggressive;

hence racial and ethnic stereotypes often coincide with the fiercest fighting in wars.[8]

Usually invented to afford great psychological and political as well as military advantages over an opponent, weapons in and of themselves seldom turn the tides of war.[9] France employed considerable new technology in its war with Prussia in 1871 but still lost. Poison gas, tanks, and machine guns were stunning and deadly innovations in World War I; yet that war ended basically as a stalemate in muddy trenches. Sometimes war winners employ sophisticated new devices, as with the atomic bombs mentioned earlier, but this does not prove that they would not still have won even without the "secret weapon." Weapons can affect the cost of war, in both personnel and resources, as much as its outcome. If we recall one of the dilemmas mentioned in the Introduction, people kill people, but guns can make it quicker and easier; or, in Senator Daniel Patrick Moynihan's play on words during congressional debates on ammunition control, "Guns don't kill people; bullets do."[10]

Most observers would agree that a nation's overall productive capability, number of useful allies, and size of skilled and mobilized populations play the greatest roles in winning wars. Weapons can make up for some deficiencies on these scores and can provide means for momentary breakthroughs, but strong and well-motivated opponents, especially those defending their own territory, have a way of coming back.

HISTORICAL PATTERNS IN THE
SPREAD OF ARMS AND ARMS TECHNOLOGY

Although arms had been dispatched from one ruler to another for many centuries, the modern beginnings of arms transfers as an organized form of diplomacy and trade have been traced, along with weapons innovations themselves, to the 1450–1650 period, first in Italy and then shifting with industrial developments and strategic war- and peacemaking to England and the Low Countries (the Netherlands), Sweden, and Germany.[11] Other historians have located the origins even somewhat earlier in the Middle Ages with the import of gunpowder into Europe in the form of Moroccan saltpeter, thus dooming the age of the crossbow and introducing the age of firearms.[12]

Both arms manufacturing and transfers grew, then, in parallel with the general development of the capitalist international economic system,[13] as engineering breakthroughs were scored and as national governments replaced local rulers in demanding larger stocks of arms. In the process, secondary arms suppliers, often in foreign countries, formed partnerships of various sorts with the older manufacturers, as in France, Russia, and Spain. Third-tier states, such as Portugal, Ottoman Turkey, Scotland,

Hungary, India, Japan, Poland, and the Balkans, also tried to copy foreign weapons. Among the increasingly widespread arms recipients or customers in the arms trade at this time were Denmark, North Africa, Persia (Iran), and Abyssinia (Ethiopia). Remarkably, we see a quite similar arms hierarchy today, including many of the same states, but with a broader array of both suppliers and recipients as well.[14]

The gap that emerged in the fifteenth century between states that had perfected the use of gunpowder and linked new scientific discoveries to warfare and those that had not generated a growing, sometimes desperate demand to catch up so as not to be outgunned by enemies. This was even the case with the doomed Indians of the American Plains—the Sioux who destroyed General George Custer's army at the Little Big Horn had acquired better and more modern rifles than had the hidebound U.S. Cavalry.

Historically, at times of relative peace and optimism, weapons innovations have slowed, only to resurge in less stable times. The rate of arms improvement and spread in world politics has not been uniform, and there have been periods of slowdown and relative stability. The 1650–1850 period was one such moment when weapons technological breakthroughs were few, even as firearms themselves became more widely available. This may have been due to the relative political moderation of the times, with conservative leaders bent on preserving their new states rather than risking aggression, at least as long as the bitter memories of the One Hundred and the Thirty Years' wars lasted. In many parts of the world soldiers were still expected to provide their own arms, as did American colonial militia, for example. As long as weapons were rather simple, the knowledge of making spears, swords, and primitive firearms was adequate and quite widespread.[15]

With the increasingly sophisticated weaponry of the Industrial Revolution, however, came a more determined, though not always successful, effort to control and profit from arms supply and to gain technological advantages over opponents. Arms still were traded and transferred widely, but the ability to design and produce them and to innovate new ones spread much more slowly.[16] Big powers, seeking both military and economic dominance, hoarded their production advantages and, even while allowing commercial partnerships with foreign manufacturers under license, did not foster widespread technological know-how.[17] When their empires began to crumble, such powers, particularly Britain, Germany, and France, were able to retain many of these production advantages over emerging new states, except ultimately for the United States and Russia/the USSR. The U.S. Civil War showed that a period of faster military-industrial innovation was beginning, with more efficient weapons such as quick-firing rifles, mobile field artillery, exploding shells, bigger naval guns, armored steamships, aerial surveillance (balloons), and so forth.[18]

Major power arms producers took advantage of wars and larger markets in selling more weapons abroad, allowing weapons firms to gain enough profits to reduce costs, hire more designers, and invest in the next generation of products. As entrepreneurs, most nineteenth-century arms inventors did not have clear plans for the use of their designs in battle; by the same token military staffs themselves were relatively slow to incorporate new equipment and adapt their tactics accordingly. Indeed, most inventors felt their weapons would make war too fearsome to be fought.[19] Arms became a primary expression of technological superiority, and the trade of weapons became one means of gaining investment capital and sustaining those technological feats.

States seeking to avoid dependence on foreign technology and entering the weapons business late had great difficulty catching up.[20] Perfection of arms design and manufacturing required chemical plants, steel mills (or secure access to them), foundries, and assembly factories—not to mention research laboratories and investment capital.[21] A full array of such resources is relatively rare and expensive; thus some reliance on foreign technology has persisted for most arms-producing countries.[22]

Since any modern arms can be lethal, however, as weapons transfers and production licenses spread in the nineteenth century, the Western powers soon were faced with increasingly troublesome political and military uprisings in less developed states—as in China's **Boxer Rebellion** at the turn of the century. The pattern of arms acquisition and development extended beyond Europe and the Americas in the late nineteenth century as states such as Japan and China sought to offset the ability of Western powers to force their way in and demand trade. The race for modern weaponry became globalized. Japanese leaders, for example, while temporarily bowing to the superior force of Admiral Matthew Perry and others in the nineteenth century, determined to preserve their country's autonomy by beating the Westerners at their own game; this came to mean arming and fighting the Russians, Europeans, Chinese, and Americans for dominance in Asia during the first half of the twentieth century and subsequently winning global nonmilitary technological competitions.

Furthermore, the spread of licensed production of one country's arms by another meant that little by little technological capabilities for producing at least basic weapons became more widely available. The early-twentieth-century arms trade was characterized by multiple firms in various countries "peddling their wares" relatively independently to foreign governments. Home governments sometimes helped subsidize weapons production and purchased arms for their own forces, but it was not uncommon for firms such as the giant British Vickers company to design and develop arms totally for export.

During World War II, however, governments became more intimately involved in arms production and transfers, as in the U.S. Lend-Lease of older naval vessels and arms to Britain and the Soviet Union. Arms firms were hitched more exclusively to the home country's war effort than they had been in World War I. Major powers came to dominate larger segments of the market for arms exports, and market shares for newly rising and revolutionary powers such as Germany, Italy, Japan, and the USSR increased markedly.[23]

For much of the early postwar period through the 1960s, arms transfers were mainly surplus and used equipment supplied free or at bargain prices to favored allies for strategic purposes. Under the Kennedy administration and Secretary of Defense Robert McNamara, however, the Pentagon decided that weapons research and development funds could be regained and U.S. allies satisfied through the government's foreign sale of more up-to-date equipment. Other major power governments, such as Britain and France, soon followed this lead, creating special weapons-selling branches in their defense ministries. Hence was born the modern push to export arms through government assistance, promotions, regulation, guarantees, and credits.

As a result of the global arms spread, certain Third World countries achieved significant military capability through foreign assistance and began infant arms industries of their own, especially—as in such cases as India or Israel—when they were considered **strategic** assets for the United States or USSR or when they were threatened with arms supply restrictions. But as the U.S.-Soviet rivalry fizzled in the 1990s, militarization by foreign assistance became somewhat more difficult. More states were left once again to gather military equipment and information from commercial sources, much as they had before World War II. Although such sources remained plentiful, customers had to offer considerable hard currency or be relatively good credit risks, and the major arms-producing states still held onto a great portion of the overall market.[24]

TODAY'S ARMS SUPPLY SYSTEM

A combination of regional conflict hot spots and the availability of funds for purchase keeps the global arms trade running. In recent years, however, it has not exactly been booming, at least as compared to the peaks of arms proliferation in the mid-1980s or during the 1970s when petrodollars (funds accumulated by the oil-exporting countries) fueled a heavy weapons demand. The fall in arms deliveries from major suppliers between 1987 and 1991 has been estimated at 55 percent. In 1990, for example, the value of global trade in major (large) conventional weapons was estimated at around $22 billion, which was less than 60 percent of the 1987 figure. The figure fell further to an estimated $18.4 billion by 1992,[25] and U.S. government data on total global (major and minor) weapons sales to the Third World in the early 1990s likewise showed the lowest levels in nearly a decade (down to about $24 billion in sales agreements).[26]

The easing of some conflicts (e.g., Iran-Iraq, Afghanistan, Angola) long driven by the cold war's superpower rivalry, the saturation of many smaller states' arms needs, and the world's general economic recession lowered arms demand. Arms production and exports were cut in a number of supplying countries because of budgetary deficits and slack import demand. Even in France, long an aspiring arms exporter that in many years ranked third in the world, weapons manufacturers complained bitterly in 1993 of disappointment that a new Conservative coalition government had failed to set aside significant new funding for arms production and export subsidy.[27]

One indicator of the pressures on arms industries was the extent of Russian production cutbacks during the political turmoil of the early 1990s, as seen in Figure 1.1. The Soviet Union had been the developing world's leading supplier in the late 1980s. The cold war's end, budgetary shortages, runaway inflation, and the desperate need to develop consumer industries resulted in vast rollback of arms production by an estimated 50–60 percent and for some weapons categories by 90 percent. Tank output, for instance, was slashed by 60 percent in 1991, and strategic missiles and aircraft by about 33 percent.[28] Tank plants turned to alternate products, such as bulldozers; old tank parts were showing up in such odd places as weight-lifting parks and gyms; and advanced plastics and composite materials formerly used for jet fighter wings found their way into wheelbarrows.[29] Nevertheless, with large arms stockpiles and pressing unemployment problems, Russian arms exports were seen as one of Moscow's best trade hopes, with relatively competitive products able to bring cash sales. Thus, Moscow stepped up its sales promotions in the international arms market, and most of the arms-manufacturing facilities remained intact.

The Soviet disintegration also at least temporarily slowed other former Eastern bloc arms exports, although the desperate need for hard currency in the former Soviet Union (FSU) and elsewhere in Eastern Europe led to renewed sales of relatively advanced previously restricted equipment (such as MiG-29 fighter jets) at bargain prices to such countries as China, Syria, and Malaysia. Indeed, a Malaysian purchase of Soviet fighter aircraft in 1993 was Russia's most successful commercial sale outside its former Eastern bloc alliance up to that time. Yet Moscow also suffered inherent disadvantages in weapons sales competition because much of its

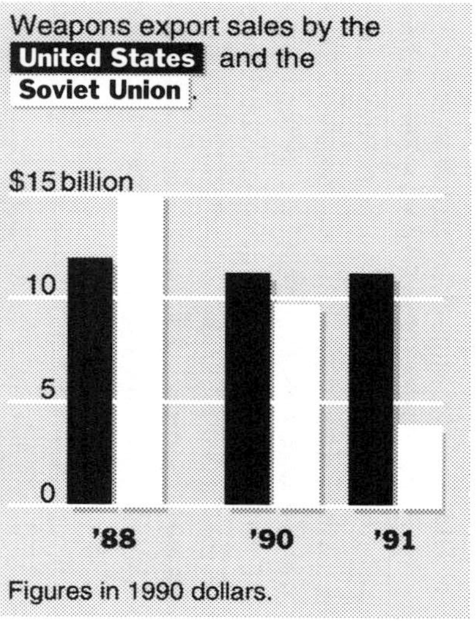

FIGURE 1.1 Leading Buyers of Russia's Arms in 1992. SOURCE: SIPRI. Reprinted in *New York Times*, February 3, 1993, p. A6. Copyright © 1993 by The New York Times Company. Reprinted by permission.

CHINA

Some $1.4 billion for 24 top-of-the-line SU-27 fighter-bombers. Also advanced S-300 surface-to-air missiles. Exploring the purchase of an aircraft carrier, MIG-31 fighter planes, diesel-powered submarines, bombers and rocket engines.

IRAN

Three diesel-powered submarines, worth about $250 million each, under a two-year-old contract signed with the Soviet Union. The first has been delivered. Twenty-four SU-24 bombers, spare parts for Iraqi planes flown to Iran for "safekeeping" during the gulf war and never returned. Unconfirmed reports of 50 MIG-29 fighter planes, MIG-31's and SU-27's, and 200 T-72 main battle tanks.

SYRIA

Reports of a $2 billion sale of 24 MIG-29's, 12 SU-27's, 300 T-72 and T-74 tanks, S-300 missiles and SA-14 shoulder-fired surface-to-air missiles.

TURKEY

Report of $75 million sale of MI-17 troop transport helicopters and BTR-60 armored personnel carriers. Also rifles.

Weapons export sales by the United States and the Soviet Union.

$15 billion / 10 / 5 / 0 — '88 '90 '91

Figures in 1990 dollars.

equipment had technological shortcomings, especially in terms of electronic controls, and uncertainties about spare parts availability. Although Russian arms remained a reasonably high-technology bargain for many Third World arms purchasers, even Malaysia hedged its aircraft purchase commitment by including an order for U.S. F-18 fighters as well.[30]

Hence, though the global arms market remained depressed, hopes for a general world move toward **disarmament** (i.e., significant arms reductions or elimination of key weapons systems) were not realized merely with the end of the U.S.-USSR rivalry. In the aftermath of the Gulf War of 1991 and the collapse of the Soviet Union, renewed arms purchase demand and sales pressures mounted. In the Middle East, for example, nearly all former Soviet equipment, including submarines, T-72 tanks, and advanced MiG-29 fighter jets, evidently could be bought for cash in the early 1990s. Washington also responded to regional market demand in the Gulf to arm clients and bolster its trade balance at the same time.[31] During 1993 the Pentagon projected weapons sales worth $28–30 billion (with deals arranged and sometimes financed through government channels), a record high surpassed only by levels in the mid-1970s (as adjusted for inflation).[32] Nevertheless, because of world economic problems, global sales were expected to remain below the peak years of the mid-1980s.

It appears (as seen in Tables 1.1 and 1.2) that the bulk of major weapon sales will continue to be concentrated among only a relatively few key clients—with the United States continuing to sell to NATO allies, wealthier Arab states, and regional powers such as Taiwan and Israel. Sales competition should be heightened, however, with several suppliers vying for NATO and other markets. Interestingly, although the Middle East's wealth and conflict potential for purchasing arms have held up relatively well, early in the 1990s the Middle East slipped at least temporarily to third place among arms-importing regions, perhaps partly because of the exhaustion of the Gulf War and the opening of regional peace talks and partly because of relatively low world oil prices, which cut into these states' income and arms-purchasing power. Also, traditionally trusted arms suppliers from the Eastern bloc were not quite as able to provide attractive terms and prices. Europe and Asia emerged as more active markets, taking 36 and 30 percent, respectively, of the world's major weapons in 1992, compared to 22 percent for the Middle East.[33] Other regions—Latin America, Africa, Oceania, North America—have continued to import only negligible shares of global arms, for reasons ranging from poverty to embargoes (South Africa), debt (Latin America, Africa), limited conflict (Latin America, Canada), and arms trade protectionism regarding domestic industries (United States).

As in prior decades, during the early 1990s the economically advanced countries of North America and Europe led the world in military spend-

TABLE 1.1 Top Ten Arms Recipients, Selected Years (million U.S. 1988 constant dollars)

| | 1963 | | | 1972 | |
	Dollar Value	% of World Total		Dollar Value	% of World Total
West Germany	1,660	14.6	South Vietnam	4,040	15.4
Indonesia	840	7.4	North Vietnam	3,030	11.6
Italy	770	6.8	West Germany	1,700	6.5
India	660	5.8	Egypt	1,390	5.3
Egypt	530	4.7	Iran	1,330	5.1
East Germany	470	4.1	South Korea	880	3.4
Iraq	380	3.3	East Germany	860	3.3
Poland	370	3.2	Israel	760	2.9
Soviet Union	330	2.9	Syria	710	2.7
South Vietnam	320	2.8	Poland	660	2.5
Total	6,330	55.6	Total	15,360	58.6

| | 1982 | | | 1988 | |
	Dollar Value	% of World Total		Dollar Value	% of World Total
Iraq	8,600	14.8	Iraq	4,600	9.5
Saudi Arabia	3,880	6.7	India	3,200	6.6
Libya	3,880	6.7	Saudi Arabia	3,000	6.2
Syria	3,150	5.4	Afghanistan	2,600	5.3
Egypt	2,300	4.0	Iran	2,000	4.1
India	2,060	3.5	Israel	1,900	3.9
Cuba	2,060	3.5	Cuba	1,700	3.5
Iran	1,940	3.3	Angola	1,600	3.3
Algeria	1,460	2.5	Vietnam	1,500	3.1
Israel	1,140	2.0	Syria	1,300	2.7
Total	30,470	52.4	Total	23,400	48.1

SOURCE: Keith Krause, *Arms and the State: Patterns of Military Production and Trade* (Cambridge: Cambridge University Press, 1992), p. 185. © Cambridge University Press 1992. Reprinted with permission of Cambridge University Press.

ing (including total military budgets), but the Third World remained the largest export market for arms. Such **less developed countries (LDCs),** struggling to satisfy social needs or build infant industries or suffering from declining export revenues, saw their share of global trade in major weapons imports slip, however, and by 1992 it was nearly equal to that of the industrialized world.[34] The trade-off between spending scarce revenues on arms or on consumer goods and investments became a political quandary for some governments, particularly for those still perceiving domestic or foreign security threats.[35]

Arms distribution among less developed countries has remained highly uneven, with most major imports going to regionally ambitious,

TABLE 1.2   Regional Acquisition of Weapons Systems, Selected Years

	1975–1976	1982–1983	1988–1989
North Atlantic Treaty Organization			
Main battle tanks	20,144	27,789	32,458
Other AFVs	35,584	58,864	71,127
Combat aircraft	11,256	10,662	11,576
Helicopters	11,169	13,617	14,699
Naval vessels	2,090	2,973	2,991
Warsaw Pact			
Main battle tanks	54,350	64,500	71,640·
Other AFVs	40,705	84,330	88,835
Combat aircraft	9,724	9,407	10,585
Helicopters	2,758	4,452	6,273
Naval vessels	2,180	2,624	2,872
Middle East and North Africa			
Main battle tanks	11,070	19,762	23,181
Other AFVs	14,311	24,342	28,818
Combat aircraft	2,594	3,621	3,921
Helicopters	884	2,307	2,209
Naval vessels	432	605	711
Sub-Saharan Africa			
Main battle tanks	500	1,962	2,186
Other AFVs	2,457	7,079	9,182
Combat aircraft	461	780	1,088
Helicopters	221	543	802
Naval vessels	164	263	253
South Asia			
Main battle tanks	2,996	4,293	5,250
Other AFVs	1,538	2,364	3,165
Combat aircraft	1,240	1,040	1,293
Helicopters	338	500	516
Naval vessels	145	155	241
East Asia			
Main battle tanks	5,250	6,870	8,829
Other AFVs	4,249	11,129	15,516
Combat aircraft	2,315	3,083	3,106
Helicopters	939	1,858	2,337
Naval vessels	982	1,253	1,938
People's Republic of China			
Main battle tanks	8,500	10,500	9,000
Other AFVs	3,600	4,600	4,800
Combat aircraft	4,340	5,980	6,730
Helicopters	350	403	463
Naval vessels	1,035	1,177	1,472
Latin America/Caribbean			
Main battle tanks	805	1,673	2,213
Other AFVs	2,245	4,615	6,996
Combat aircraft	940	1,118	1,279
Helicopters	601	941	1,025
Naval vessels	500	588	574

SOURCE: Keith Krause, *Arms and the State: Patterns of Military Production and Trade* (Cambridge: Cambridge University Press, 1992), p. 189. © Cambridge University Press 1992. Reprinted with the permission of Cambridge University Press.

"IT'S...UH... NICE, BUT WHERE DO WE SLEEP?"

Arms sales and development needs of Third World countries. Carol* Simpson/Rothco.

conflict-prone, or better-funded states in the Middle East and Asia (India, Pakistan, Saudi Arabia, Egypt, Israel, Syria, Afghanistan, Iran, the Koreas, Thailand, and Taiwan).[36] Many of these were classified as **newly industrializing countries (NICs),** and some were developing their own weapons-producing capabilities.

Certain notable arms importers of the 1980s—Iraq, Libya, Israel, and Kuwait—for a variety of reasons diminished their purchases significantly in the early 1990s, indicating that arms demand is never constant. It is subject to economic ups and downs, embargoes and boycotts (such as the one applied by the international community to Iraq, Jordan, and Kuwait in 1990), budget reductions, the completion of individual countries' arms acquisition cycles (armed forces can use or absorb only so much at a time), government change, and shifts from war to peace. Different regions also appear to import different combinations of weapons (Table 1.2), some stressing tanks; others, helicopters, patrol boats, or fast vehicles.

One final key factor affecting demand for arms imports is a country's ability to become more self-reliant, to develop its own arms industries at least for some key weapons or parts. Past embargoes have stimulated such **indigenous** production efforts by Israel, Argentina, Brazil, South Africa, Chile, and India, among others. Greater self-reliance, however, also usually entails significant continued import of parts and key weapon components and thus continued dependence, at least to some degree, on outside powers.

In the early years of the cold war, the 1950s and 1960s, most states not in a major power's alliance—that is, Third World states—remained highly dependent on one principal major power arms supplier. Often this was their former colonial ruler, as in the case of British supplies to India. However, partly because of a fear of becoming overly dependent and therefore vulnerable to political manipulation and control through embargoes, and partly because of the search for reasonably priced weapons and components, gradually more and more arms-importing states diversified their weapon suppliers. This strategy became practical as more weapons-manufacturing countries emerged and as the push to export weapons for commercial interests developed in the 1970s. By 1991, only 31 out of more than 120 arms-purchasing countries in the world were getting their arms solely from Western or Eastern bloc suppliers, and except for the United Kingdom and Cuba, these tended to be small states with no great military purchases. In other words, most nations today purchase arms from varied sources and are not limited by ideology or alliance ties.[37]

Some customers, such as Israel and Syria, still demand large quantities of highly advanced equipment and for political and economic reasons are forced to rely primarily on the United States or Russia, along with a few substitute sources such as the Czech Republic, China, Slovakia, or the Koreas. However, as more Third World states have fought their own battles and developed more of their own technical skills, the benefits of close ties to a primary major power arms source have been offset by the flexibility and lower economic costs of shopping around. Of course, if a sudden traumatic invasion or crisis occurs, as it did for Kuwait and Saudi Arabia when Iraq attacked in 1990, there might be no substitute for reliance on a major power or a coalition of such powers.

Therefore, the arms "supply side" continues to be dominated by major powers and especially the United States. The former Soviet Union and other European powers remain key exporters, but generally on a somewhat reduced scale. In 1990, the United States and Soviet Union still accounted for nearly 70 percent of major arms exports, leaving an additional 20 percent for the European Community (particularly France, Britain, and Germany), nearly 8 percent for China, and a little more than 1 percent for other NIC arms exporters (such as Brazil, North Korea, and Israel, which is both an arms customer and seller).[38] When all weapons transfers, not just major arms, were tallied, by 1992 the United States alone stood atop the export league with a 57 percent market share, three times that of the FSU, while France and China had nearly 3 percent between them. Nevertheless, by 1993 Moscow was openly aiming to regain its former market dominance.

The major powers still enjoy a **comparative advantage** in weapons supply (i.e., they produce weapons with more efficiency and at lower cost than other states and, in some cases, than they themselves can produce other types of goods) since they tend to manufacture high volumes and a full range of land, sea, and air equipment. They also offer technical assistance, financial credits, and the guarantee of weapons battle tested or at least fully evaluated by their own armed forces.

On the whole, much of the increase in supplier interest in selling weapons has been for economic, rather than strategic, motives. In the 1980s, China especially began to supply advanced designs, such as missile technologies, at relatively low prices, a form of arms proliferation that worries the other major powers. NICs in the 1980s enjoyed marked success in exporting arms designed for certain specific markets, such as light planes, fast attack patrol boats, armored personnel carriers, and fighting vehicles; in specialized designs, for example, Brazil and others utilized a "keep it simple, keep it cheap" approach in designing equipment for desert warfare. But these states' market share proved to be soft and highly vulnerable; when key customers such as Iraq could no longer pay for imports, Brazilian arms industries went bankrupt.

Ironically, a new arms control agreement, the 1989 **Conventional Forces in Europe (CFE) Agreement,** which closely restricted the number of arms to be deployed on the Continent, resulted in enough excess equipment in Western Europe to saturate the Third World market.[39] Such saturation and competition for sales threaten the profit margins of arms manufacturers and result in numerous pressures on them and on governments (see Box 1.1).

EMERGING TRENDS IN ARMS SUPPLY

Even though traditional and new combinations of suppliers and recipients remain, several additional trends are apparent in the flow of international arms. Because of cost and other factors, sales of complete weapons systems, such as jet planes and tanks, have somewhat given way to sales of components that can be assembled on the spot or combined with systems from other countries to enhance existing weapon designs at lower cost. This arrangement relieves purchasing countries of the need to be constantly buying new top-of-the-line equipment and also allows them partially to conceal the ultimate design of their weapons. For example, South Africa, long under an international arms embargo, has become adept at adding to or modifying designs, so-called **retrofitting,** utilizing var-

BOX 1.1 The Arms Supermarket

Arms customers that can afford to pay (as opposed to relying on credits or grants) now have the luxury of shopping freely among both Western and Eastern suppliers, with relatively few questions asked by exporters about the ultimate use of the weapons. Traditionally pro-Western clients such as the United Arab Emirates and Turkey, along with formerly anti-Soviet states such as Iran, have even picked up Soviet equipment at bargain prices. In 1991–1992 NATO member Turkey, after buying former East German helicopters and other equipment from the reunified Germany, reportedly turned directly to Moscow for purchases after the Germans raised questions about Turkey's crackdown on its Kurdish ethnic minority. Iran startled the West by buying Russian submarines and aircraft in 1992, whereas China was reportedly negotiating with Ukraine to purchase an aircraft carrier. Even ideological or religious differences do not necessarily preclude deals in the weapons business. "It is much harder to track the flow of former Soviet arms since the centralized Soviet state evaporated and 15 sovereign countries emerged, each with a chunk of the Soviet army and each with a need for hard currency." Despite careful controls, some worried that Soviet nuclear weapons might find their way into the Third World in the same way.

In recent wars, most notably the ten-year-long Iran-Iraq struggle of the 1980s, many suppliers shipped weapons to both sides. Some two dozen countries supplied Iraq, for example, and a good number of these—France, China, and the United States, among others—also sent at least some weapons to Iran. Partly, this might have been by political design—to keep the war stalemated or to gain desired political concessions, as in the famous U.S. Iran-contra arms fiasco. In the convoluted strategies of the latter case, the Reagan administration attempted at once to gain funds for anti-Marxist Nicaraguan rebels by selling arms to Iran, defying congressional bans in the process, in the vain hope also of freeing U.S. hostages held by pro-Iranian forces in Lebanon. Partly as well, sales to both sides provided more trade revenues to the arms exporters.

SOURCES: Michael Collins Dunn, "At the 'End of History,' the Arms Bazaar Becomes a Yard Sale," *Washington Post Report on Middle East Affairs* 13 (August-September 1992): 20, 91; Frederic S. Pearson, Michael Brzoska, and Christer Crantz, "The Effects of Arms Transfers on Wars and Peace Negotiations," in *SIPRI Yearbook 1992: World Armaments and Disarmament* (Oxford: Oxford University Press, 1992), Ch. 10.

ious parts. Sometimes these modified systems are **reexported** for profit to countries with specialized defense needs.

It is relatively easy to acquire components suitable for weapons production and evade restrictions or embargoes since certain types of products, such as electronic or automotive equipment, are often classified as having **dual use** for both civilian and military production. The discovery of Saddam Hussein's nuclear weapons development program and a supposed Iraqi "supergun" project (to be made from specialized ultralong steel pipe able to fire a projectile that conceivably could have reached Israel) pointed up the proliferation of dual use components. In the nuclear field alone, computers, detonators, centrifuges, and weapons-grade fuels all were procured relatively easily, though sometimes illegally, from Western countries and companies. Of course, not all countries that obtain such materials aim to make nuclear bombs or superguns, which raises the dilemma of identifying true security risks. Numerous restrictions are in place or are being proposed on trade of **strategic materials**—natural resources or basic products useful in the defense industry—but companies and even governments have often looked the other way in the interest of commercial gain.

As demand for high-technology arms has grown, especially with the evident U.S. successes using such equipment during the 1991 Gulf War, cash-strapped governments have turned to **diversification** strategies (i.e., the purchase of arms from a variety of sources) and makeshift designs and add-ons to upgrade their armaments and imitate Western arms technology at lower cost.[40] It appears that the side that scans and controls the battlefield electronically (from satellites or high-flying aircraft) has a distinct advantage. So-called smart self-guided weapons of high accuracy promise to make devastating "surgical" strikes against opponents in air-to-air and air-to-ground or surface-to-surface (naval) combat with relatively little risk to the striking force's own personnel. With this push toward high-tech arms, the arms trade of the future may involve more intellectual property (designs, know-how, patents, licenses, computer control software, etc.) than hardware, as could be seen in Russia's 1993 technology transfer pact with China.[41]

At times the advantages afforded by the most advanced and exotic equipment have been exaggerated; smart weapons seem never quite as good as advertised, and **collateral damage** (destruction of surrounding property and innocent people) usually accompanies any surgical raids. Few states can hope to attain the technology levels of the latest electronic and laser equipment, but a growing number appear to strive for improved guided missiles and some greater air and antitank defense capabilities. China and North Korea, for example, have been crucial to upgrading Iranian, Pakistani, and Syrian missile attack options; Israel and India have

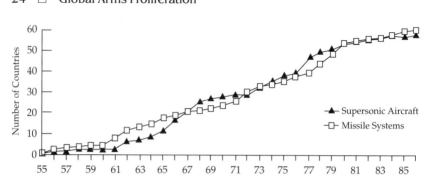

FIGURE 1.2 The Spread of Supersonic Aircraft and Missiles to Less Developed Countries, 1955–1985

Note: Missile systems include fixed and mobile surface-to-surface and surface-to-air systems, air-to-air, and air-to-surface missiles on fighter aircraft and on helicopters, and anti-tank, ship-to-ship, and ship-to-air missiles. SOURCE: Christian Catrina, *Arms Transfers and Dependence* (New York: Taylor and Francis/UNIDIR, 1988), p. 28, using SIPRI data.

worked feverishly to maintain their regional advantages in ballistic missile launch capabilities.[42]

Another clear trend since the 1960s has been the steady advance in *sophistication*, if not numbers, of weapons transferred. Figure 1.2 roughly indicates the pace of such advances in the aerospace field, for example, by detailing the number of countries possessing supersonic jet fighters and various forms of guided missiles. A big jump occurred in the late 1970s, and the numbers continued to creep upward, to more than sixty countries, in the 1980s. In addition to transfers, many countries now have a record of manufacturing various forms of ballistic missiles, as seen in Table 1.3. Of course, the bulk of the spread of weapons and manufacturing know-how still involves relatively short-range and often rather inaccurate equipment, but in a remarkable increase of available firepower by the mid-1980s, 52 LDCs had become capable of some level of military production, 55 LDCs had acquired supersonic aircraft, 71 had tactical missiles, 107 fielded armored fighting vehicles, and 81 had modern warships.[43]

The implications of such technological proliferation are still being debated. Some argue that higher-tech weapons make their users more, rather than less, dependent on the major power suppliers, especially in the heat of battle. More sophisticated weapons can increase the rate of **attrition,** or equipment destruction and breakdowns in battle, requiring more training, replacement units, and parts and thus increasing the leverage of the arms supplier over the client.[44] For example, despite rather advanced air forces, neither Saudi Arabia nor Kuwait alone was a match for Iraq without significant U.S. and European support. Partly this was due to

TABLE 1.3 Countries with Record of Missile Manufacturing, 1990

Type of Missile	Countries Possessing This Type
Air to air	Brazil, China, France, Israel, Italy, Japan, South Africa, Taiwan, U.K., U.S., USSR (CIS)
Air to ground	Argentina, Brazil, France, Germany, Israel, U.K., U.S., USSR (CIS)
Anti-armor/antitank	Argentina, Brazil, China, France, Germany, India, Israel, Italy, Japan, Spain, Sweden, Switzerland, U.K., U.S., USSR (CIS), technology shared in multinational production
Antiship	Brazil, China, France, Germany, Italy, U.K., Israel, Japan, Norway, Sweden, Taiwan, U.S., USSR (CIS)
Antisubmarine	Australia, France, Italy, U.S., USSR (CIS)
Battlefield support guided	Argentina, Brazil, China, France, India, Iraq, Israel, Pakistan, Taiwan, U.S., USSR (CIS)
Strategic land based and sea based	China, France, India, U.S., USSR (CIS)
Surface to air	Brazil, China, Egypt, France, Germany, India, Israel, Italy, Japan, Pakistan, Sweden, Switzerland, Taiwan, U.K., U.S. (shared with NATO technology), USSR (CIS)
Theater (regional) cruise	U.S., USSR (CIS)

SOURCE: Gregory R. Copley, ed., *Defense and Foreign Affairs Handbook, 1990–1991* (Alexandria, VA: International Media Corp., 1990).

lack of personnel; size and motivation of forces still play a decisive military role in battle, for which not even advanced military equipment can fully compensate.

Thus, the supposedly greater independence afforded by acquiring or developing sophisticated arms from a variety of sources can be an illusion. Yet states also seek such sophistication for battlefield advantages and for prestige. Iraq for one is thought to have benefited from technological armament superiority in holding off Iran's larger forces for many years during the two countries' Gulf confrontation in the 1980s.

There are, then, essentially two tiers in today's world of weapons. The major powers have maintained their lead in developing big ticket, advanced military hardware. These include all forms of nuclear strategic systems and launch vehicles, though the numbers of these weapons have been decreased by agreements among the two largest powers and by reduced tensions among some of the others. Sophisticated air frame, jet engine, naval, and electronics technologies also remain largely within the province of the major powers, although increasingly even advanced European states are heavily strained to stay in the top echelon of military technology.[45] Less developed states are greatly outspent in this area and must produce equipment partly with foreign components and find segments of the market overlooked or neglected by the developed states.

One of the troubling aspects of the current arms market is the growing array of suppliers and equipment. Although sales have had fits and starts, and in the last decade generally have sagged,[46] the potential for continual arms proliferation is clearly evident. We see equipment available for international exchange ranging from small arms to sophisticated top-of-the-line systems as well as imitations and specialty products in between. As one example, because the East German regime needed hard currency in its last days, it sold the latest portable antitank and other Warsaw Pact weapons to the West, with few or no ideological questions asked about whether the weapons might ultimately threaten East Germany's own forces.[47]

Since the international arms market is segmented, some advanced or favored customers import more potent systems than other less wealthy or strategically favored states. As in automobile sales, there is a trickle-down effect, with older or lower-tech armament models sold off to buyers further down the economic hierarchy as state-of-the-art equipment becomes available at the top. Used weapons dealers supplement intergovernmental transactions by gathering large lots of surplus equipment and re-transferring them to governments or political groups, sometimes at the behest of intelligence agencies such as the U.S. Central Intelligence Agency (CIA) or the State Security Agency (KGB) in Moscow.[48]

Wars in one region generate surplus supplies that can be sold off to other areas, thus precipitating a contagion effect as the weapons from one war potentially fuel another. One of the primary sources of weapons to factions in the 1992 Yugoslavian civil war, for example, were political factions from the decades-old Lebanese conflict.[49] Weapons from the Yugoslav fighting subsequently were shipped (and at least partially intercepted en route) to Somalia. Long wars, such as those in the Middle East, Southeast Asia, and Africa, often cause such economic damage that arms trading becomes a highly lucrative source of income for groups of fighters and traders. Gun running was reputed to be rampant among tribal fighters involved in the long Afghan civil war of the 1980s, and many have worried about arms sell-offs by cash-starved troops in the former Soviet Union.

CONCLUSION

This, then, is the state of weapons proliferation and use as the century draws to a close: Over the past three decades, arms transfers have evolved from mostly giveaways of older and obsolete equipment to cash-and-credit commercially driven sales of more up-to-date designs. One relatively optimistic summary notes that "worldwide the military sector is shrinking. Democratic regimes are replacing military rulers. Defense spending is down. Military industries are going out of business. Defense production is declining, military assistance is dwindling, and the arms trade has contracted dramatically."[50] Yet arms suppliers still ply their wares on the global market; certain ambitious regional powers are involved in continuing arms races; newer arms technologies are spreading; ethnic warfare is raging.

In subsequent chapters, the motivations and methods involved in these emerging trends are explored, as are possible ways to manage or limit proliferation. Clearly, however, today more countries have more varied and advanced types of equipment from more numerous suppliers. Yet the rate of acquisition has slowed for most customers, and certain arms suppliers, especially the smaller ones, have had difficulty maintaining a market share. We must understand both the political and economic forces behind the arms trade if we are to have any hope of drafting policies, agreements, or regulations to manage it or control its effects in the future. The modern weapons economy has become intricately woven into our overall economies and increasingly multinationalized.

The structure of global arms proliferation reviewed in this chapter raises both dilemmas of causation and access, that is, questions of whether arms cause wars and whether it is any longer reasonable or fair for each country to assert a sovereign right to arm. To answer these questions, we must better define the modes of arms transfers existing today and determine the reasons for and consequences of such transfers. This task relates both to arms production and trade, two key forms of economic activity in today's world. The human impetus to invent, exchange, and improve armament is discussed in the next chapter, as are the dilemmas of alternatives and adequacy—how governments have used armament to struggle, perhaps in vain, for both economic welfare and military security.

TWO

□ □ □

The Impetus to Manufacture
and Acquire Arms

The previous historical review of trends in the global spread of arms highlighted the close connection between arms manufacturing and export. Arms exports are in effect the sale of excess production in order to finance continued production. The extent and reasons for that production, which drives the global spread of arms, are the focus of this chapter.

As we saw in Chapter 1, it would be too easy to conclude that military preparations and expenditures are sweeping the world. Some studies nevertheless maintain that the long-term sweep has been nearly out of control and cite data showing that absolute amounts of military spending have soared, doubling and redoubling in the twentieth century.[1] Yet when the general growth of economies is controlled for and the comparative rates of growth between the military and other economic sectors are measured, the share of the global economy going to military pursuits has shrunk during recent times. This decline has been relatively uniform for both advanced and less developed countries (see Figure 2.1) but perhaps has been most striking among Western developed states, which seem to have reached "maturity" in the size of their military establishments. Marxist and Islamic states, in a sense trying to catch up in terms of power, have continued to invest more in the military.[2]

Generally as countries grow wealthier over time, their available budget funds increase, and military expenditures and mobilization rise accordingly, whether or not the military exerts greater influence over the society or political decisionmaking (the latter often referred to as rising **militarism**).[3] But studies also have shown that militarism matters, especially for the acquisition of arms and the global arms trade. In some countries arms purchase decisions are dominated by the military "top brass." Often the bulk of military spending goes for personnel and upkeep,[4] so that factors such as military influence on the government become crucial in tipping the balance or winning debates about weapon development or purchase decisions versus other priorities.

FIGURE 2.1 Development of Military Expenditures, 1981–1991
SOURCE: Herbert Wulf, "Arms Industry Limited: The Turning Point in the 1990s," in *Arms Industry Limited*, ed. Herbert Wulf (Oxford: Oxford University Press, 1993), p. 4, courtesy of SIPRI.

For example, countries that in the 1970s and 1980s produced and imported the most arms included those that spent large proportions of their gross national product (GNP) on defense, those that possessed relatively great disposable income, and those—such as Iraq, Iran, Israel, Syria, Libya, India, Pakistan, Taiwan, and the Koreas—that had developed ambitious military buildup goals extending into new technologies, including in many cases nuclear technology. An overall pattern of both military growth and effort and lingering international political conflict, rather than involvement in any specific foreign war, characterized such major arms importers.

A military ambition and threat perception factor therefore appears to combine with greater economic wealth (in the Third World often based on oil resources) as the driving forces behind the acquisition of arms. Traditional, cultural, and even emotional or ideological views of the military, or of foreign or domestic security threats, also appear to condition states' overall military effort and spending.[5]

THE ARMS MAKERS AND SUPPLIERS

A wide variety of actors are involved in arms production, and therefore the interests and policies involved in that enterprise are both complex and a bit obscure. There is a close connection between government and mili-

TABLE 2.1 International Arms Market: Actors and Objectives

Actors	Objectives
National Actors	
Nation-states and national governmental authorities	Security, political influence, economic growth, solvency, full employment, budgetary allocations
Subnational Actors	
Industrial and corporate units	Maximum economic gain—profits in market economies or budgetary allocations in controlled economies
Techno-scientific centers (research groups, universities, institutes)	Service for military and private sector, new knowledge, techniques, products, and funding
Separate governmental bureaucracies	Surveillance and control of other subnationals, budgetary allocations
Financial institutions (banks, etc.)	Return on loans, government influence
Transnational Actors	
Multinational corporations and banks	Maximum economic gain, political influence
Revolutionary movements	Political change/power
International Actors	
Military alliances	Deterrence, collective influence, protection of dependent states
Economic or political communities (e.g., EC)	Trade and technological competitiveness, political coordination
World and regional organizations	Regional order, development, arms control

SOURCE: Adapted from Christian Catrina, *Arms Transfers and Dependencies* (New York: Taylor and Francis/UNIDIR, 1988), p. 69.

tary representatives, on the one hand, and civilian arms manufacturers and distributors, on the other.

Table 2.1 lists these various actors and their basic objectives in the "weapons game." Some of them are found at the national or subnational level and include interest groups such as manufacturers or financiers looking to gain profit from the arms trade. Others are **transnational actors,** which operate across national boundaries and include multinational corporations, with subsidiaries or outlets in many countries, or groups of terrorists, looking to acquire deadly weapons, and international governmental (e.g., the United Nations) and nongovernmental (e.g., the Union of Concerned Scientists) organizations that sometimes seek to control or keep track of the arms trade. Among the most powerful transnational groupings are **consortia,** or international partnerships, of manufacturers pooling resources to market weapons.

Since arms manufacturing and exports are a form of big business, many of these national and multinational actors can be seen promoting weapon

BOX 2.1 Inside the Paris Air Show, 1991

To whet the appetites of those Middle Easterners and other customers for state-of-the-art military technology, organizers invited 80 defense ministries to attend what was proudly described as the largest show ever, with 1,769 exhibitors from 38 countries, 51,600 square meters of exhibition space, and 212 aircraft on display. The main exhibit hall, a massive airplane hangar several football fields in length, was filled wall-to-wall with manufacturers' displays of everything from executive jets to electronic warfare devices. The tarmac outside held scores of aircraft on "static display," neatly grouped by country of origin. A record 465 companies and governments erected "chalets" that lined the main runway—elegant entertainment suites built especially for the occasion—places to wine and dine potential customers while they watched flight demonstrations. ...

Videos were big; many exhibitors put together tapes of their own "greatest hits." McDonnell Douglas's press center continuously screened an elaborate video with a squadron of Apache helicopters taking off to the strains of "Amazing Grace," heading out to destroy Iraqi tanks and take Iraqi soldiers prisoner. ...

The most sophisticated video display was an interactive terminal operated by the U.S. Air Force. Passersby could choose from a "menu" of U.S. aircraft. At the press of a button, the viewer was treated to scenes ranging from a test flight of the new Advanced Technology Fighter to combat footage of the Stealth fighter making "pinpoint" bombing runs in Iraq. All the bombs in the air force video were on target, just like those seen on TV during the war, and none of the footage showed anyone being killed or wounded by this high-tech onslaught.

SOURCE: William Hartung, "The Boom at the Arms Bazaar," *Bulletin of the Atomic Scientists* 47, no. 8 (October 1991): 14. From the *Bulletin of the Atomic Scientists.* Copyright © 1991 by the Educational Foundation for Nuclear Science, 6042 South Kimbark, Chicago, IL 60637, USA. A one-year subscription to the *Bulletin* is $30.

sales at annual or biannual international arms expositions, fairs, and air shows, such as those near London and Paris (see Box 2.1). These extravaganzas rival auto and boat shows for spectacular displays of goods, complete with glamorous models (humans and products), videos, and hype.[6]

Manufacturing firms, both large corporations and small subcontractors, vie for production contracts and orders. Their sales staffs hobnob with military personnel from many countries; sales agents and "middlemen," for a fee, also help bring buyers and sellers together (occasionally using illegal influence). Military staff attachés stationed in foreign embassies frequently take part in such sales promotions. Civilian government officials oversee the terms of agreements and financing to make sure licensing and other regulations are observed, at least minimally, and to guarantee against default in payments.

In addition to the high-ranking individuals closing the arms deals, many other actors are involved behind the scenes in the weapons business. As seen in Table 2.2, large numbers of workers and engineers are employed in the defense sectors of leading arms-producing countries by both prime and subcontractors—which in major powers such as the United States can number into the tens of thousands—producing everything from ammunition to the control display panels for electronic equipment. Market slowdowns in the late 1980s began taking a toll on this employment, however.[7]

As significant as such jobs might be to various countries and regions, they still represent only a small fraction of the employment totals in most advanced economies, such as that of the United States, Japan, or Western Europe. Nevertheless, because of this production, trade unions and interest groups gain a stake in the defense industry. Towns and cities come to depend on the payrolls, and national and local political officials play a role in promoting the industry, especially in the United States, where the Pentagon has followed a traditional policy of awarding contracts and facilities to nearly every county and congressional district. The **military-industrial complex,** a term coined by President Dwight Eisenhower in his 1961 farewell address to warn of excess demands and concentrated political-economic power by influential corporate and military elites, is also evident abroad. In the early 1990s, Russia, for example, inherited a Soviet defense industry of seventeen hundred companies, two hundred research centers, and six million workers and immediately had to confront the daunting challenge of finding alternate employment for these workers in a consumer economy.[8]

In most arms-producing states, major weapons usually are produced under government "procurement contracts" to supply the armed forces. Designs can be specified ahead of time by the military or defense departments, or companies can develop new designs to compete in tests to win government purchase. Such competition even existed in the USSR, where various state-owned weapons design "labs," led by prominent aeronautical engineers, produced prototype weapons—the famous MiG (Mikoyan), Antonov, Sukhoi, Tupolev, and Ilyushin aircraft, for example. As part of what can be termed **industrial policy,** major power governments often parcel out contracts to various manufacturers and labs in order to keep them in business. Thus, Washington has sustained numerous aerospace firms (McDonnell Douglas, Northrop, Boeing, General Dynamics, Lockheed, etc.), while other countries have pared down to one or two.

Government contracts generally specify weapon cost targets and guidelines, though in practice these often are exceeded to some extent under **cost-plus** (added expense allowed) provisions. Close consultation among government project managers, military officers, and manufacturers' rep-

TABLE 2.2   Global Arms Industry Employment, 1980s–1992

Country	Early 1980s	Mid-1980s	1990–1992[a]
Former Soviet Union	5,800,000	6,000,000	5,900,000
Russia	–	–	4,500,000
Ukraine	–	–	800,000
Belarus	–	–	150,000
Kazakhstan	–	–	75,000
Baltic Republics	–	–	100,000
All other former Soviet republics	–	–	275,000
China	4,000,000	–	3,000,000–5,000,000
USA	2,085,000	3,100,000	2,750,000
UK	560,000	470,000	(400,000)[b]
France	340,000	290,000	255,000
Germany	268,000	347,000	241,000
Former West	268,000	307,000	200,000
Former East	–	40,000	41,000
India	235,000	240,000	250,000
Poland	–	260,000	180,000
Spain	(40,000)	66,000	100,000
Romania	–	–	90,000
Italy	78,000	86,000	80,000
South Africa	100,000	100,000	(80,000)
Czechoslovakia	–	145,000	75,000
Egypt	75,000	100,000	75,000
Israel	90,000	90,000	60,000
North Korea	55,000	–	(55,000)
Canada	46,000	(50,000)	50,000
Pakistan	40,000	50,000	(50,000)
Yugoslavia	–	–	(50,000)
Japan	33,000	39,000	45,000
Iran	–	–	45,000
Brazil	75,000	75,000	(40,000)

(*continues*)

resentatives is maintained throughout production. Manufacturers come to rely on government both for research and development funds to design and produce weapons and for assistance in marketing them abroad.

Clearly the hub of this network is the weapons-manufacturing firm. These can be privately or publicly owned companies, either specializing completely in arms production or dabbling in it for a portion of their business. The larger the conglomerate firm, the more likely that it will undertake both military and civilian production; diversified companies probably are more able to survive cuts in military spending than those wholly dependent on defense contracts, but they may be less expert in defense as opposed to civilian production.

Through the historical development of the international arms market, close relations *and* subtle conflicts developed between governments and

TABLE 2.2 (*continued*)

Country	Early 1980s	Mid-1980s	1990–1992[a]
Taiwan	50,000	–	(40,000)
South Korea	30,000	–	(40,000)
Sweden	29,000	35,000	30,000
Hungary	–	–	30,000
Belgium	20,000–30,000	35,000	25,000
Switzerland	–	30,000	25,000
Turkey	–	–	(25,000)
Indonesia	26,000	–	(25,000)
Netherlands	13,000	18,000	(20,000)
Singapore	11,000	–	20,000
Argentina	60,000	(60,000)	20,000
Greece	–	15,000	14,000
Australia	–	–	12,000
Norway	–	15,000	10,000
Portugal	–	–	10,000
Finland	–	–	10,000
Chile	3,000	–	(10,000)
Denmark	–	–	7,000
Peru	5,000	–	(5,000)
Philippines	5,000	–	(5,000)
Thailand	5,000	–	(5,000)
Malaysia	3,000	–	(5,000)
New Zealand	–	–	500
Iraq	–	–	–
Syria	–	–	–
Saudi Arabia	–	–	–

[a]Countries are listed in order of their employment figures for 1990–1992, column 4.

[b]Figures in parentheses are estimates.

SOURCE: Herbert Wulf, "Arms Industry Limited: The Turning Point in the 1990s," in *Arms Industry Limited*, ed. Herbert Wulf (Oxford: Oxford University Press, 1993), pp. 14–15, courtesy of SIPRI.

weapons-manufacturing firms. On the one hand, firms were treated as valuable national assets whose contracts and sales were promoted and encouraged. On the other hand, they were also seen as potential security threats, which if allowed to sell weapons indiscriminately abroad to potential enemies could undermine the home country's defenses. Manufacturers in turn could pressure governments to accept more new weapons than they might have wanted in order both to keep the firm in business and available for wartime and to procure weapons at least as advanced as those being sold to foreigners.

Although arms producers suffered a major blow after World War I, when war critics labeled them "merchants of death," even early in this century the beginnings of the military-industrial complex were evident.[9] Certain firms even took on the trappings of dynasties. One of the most remarkable was the Krupp steel conglomerate of Germany, a company with a four-centuries-long history in the same extended family (its main initial product was spoons). Krupp slowly geared up for the peak of arms production in the nineteenth and early-to-mid-twentieth centuries.[10] As with so many of the world's major arms producers, weapons always constituted only a portion of Krupp's turnover; indeed profits from commercial production were often used to finance weapons research. Krupp was fortified by its selection as Prussia's main armorer on the eve of the Franco-Prussian War of 1870, though the company's sales continued to extend broadly to other countries, including Russia. In a pattern to be repeated many times by many firms, Krupp ignition fuses were used by both sides in World War I.

Krupp also showed a persistent ability to survive commercially through political connections, demonstrating that in the arms business ideologies and philosophies do not necessarily mean much. When Germany was forbidden weapons after World War I, Krupp nonetheless continued to develop them secretly, taking advantage of production ties to the young Marxist Soviet Union.[11] Found guilty of war crimes at the Nuremburg trials following World War II for having used slave labor from nearby Nazi concentration camps, Alfried Krupp nevertheless was able to preserve the firm, though reducing its stake in the arms business, by cooperating with the Western allies in the cold war against communism. He sold products widely both to NATO and the Third World before selling the company itself to a limited stock corporation in 1968.[12]

The great private arms firms also had their government-owned counterparts in many countries, including Britain's Royal Ordnance Factories (which was finally privatized, i.e., opened for public stock offerings, by the Thatcher government in the 1980s). Traditionally most of the world's arms have been produced by such nationalized firms since most governments see arms production as too sensitive and threatening to be left entirely to private business decisions. Only the advanced Western economies, specifically that of the United States, as yet have had sufficient domestic capital to allow arms production to fall primarily into private hands. Even then production has been nurtured by government contracts and limited by government regulation. In the developing world, domestic capital for such privately driven arms production is lacking, and arms generally are either bought from abroad or produced by government-owned enterprises able to concentrate scarce capital on national security projects.[13]

Along with weapons designers and manufacturers, successful private arms dealers also emerged centuries ago to facilitate weapons transfers among countries. Many of these agents came to trade mainly in used weaponry, a tradition still carried on by firms such as the multinational

Interarms, Inc. It is owned by the legendary Sam Cummings, an American living, reputedly for tax purposes, in Switzerland and doing business from regional offices and a fortified headquarters building—resistant to raids by the Irish Republican Army (IRA)—in Manchester, England. The nineteenth-century firm Bannerman and Sons was the first U.S. dealer of this type, originating in 1865 with the surplus of Civil War arms, just as Cummings originally entered the business dealing surplus World War II armament (in cooperation with the CIA).

Dealers can be either aboveboard or clandestine. Interarms, for example, claims to sell weapons only through legal channels (i.e., with permits) to governments, groups, and individuals for purposes ranging from sports and collecting to warfare. Bannerman's catalog explained, "The Good Book says that in the millennium days, swords shall be turned into plowshares and spears into pruning hooks. We are helping to hasten the glad time by selling cannon balls to heal the sick."[14] (The next chapter deals further with the covert and illegal sides of the arms trade.)

The Appendix lists 100 of today's foremost arms manufacturers, along with the extent and pattern of their defense production and total profits. The arms business has been attractive mainly because it has traditionally provided a handsome return on investments. Only 12 of the world's top 100 manufacturers reporting data in 1989 failed to make an overall profit, though with slumping markets their combined arms production fell that year by 4 percent; in 1990, 20 companies reported losses. The biggest firms have been highly concentrated in just fourteen countries, with an obvious dominance by the major Western powers; for example in 1989, 47 U.S. corporations accounted for 63 percent of the total major weapon sales.[15] As seen in the Appendix, the business volume conducted by some of these corporate giants rivals the GNPs of some countries.

In addition to the profits and employment levels just noted, in the case of the United States and FSU as well as other powers, advanced defense technology has meant sustained exports when other trade sectors were dying out. Partly this success can be attributed to directed government research and development investments, making very costly weapon systems easier, less risky, and cheaper to produce. There is a **learning curve** in arms production, meaning costs per weapon tend to go down with longer and longer production runs as processes are learned and **economies of scale** (the concept of "cheaper by the dozen") set in. Thus, when government agencies can guarantee purchase of large numbers of weapons for their armed forces, they help manufacturers reduce costs per unit produced and increase profits. Export markets, expanding sales and thereby production, can also increase such profits, depending upon prices. Government agencies often assist in arranging and financing such exports, reasoning that they help sustain industrial employment and re-

TABLE 2.3   Prices for Russian Military Hardware for Sale in 1993 at a Major Weapons Market in Ukraine

Commodity	Production Date	Price (in US$)
MiG-27 fighter plane	1988–1990	16 million
Yakovlev-28 bomber	1985–1988	13 million
Sukhoi-27SK fighter plane	New	31 million
Ilyushin-76TD transport plane	New	32 million
Mi-24 combat helicopter	New	7 million
S-300V anti-aircraft system	New	650,000
T-80V tank	New	2.2 million
R-3305 radio jammer	New	30,300
123mm howitzer	1968–1974	50,000
Kilo-class diesel submarine	1992	130,000
BTR-8S armored personnel carrier	New	300,337
Strela-10M missile	New	30,000

SOURCE: Richard Boudreaux, "Attention Shoppers." Reprinted by permission of *Los Angeles Times*.

duce the cost of arms for the country's own forces. Long-term effects on the nation's total economy and the effect of arms on global security and insecurity may not be so readily calculated, however.

Arms export prices appear to fluctuate according to market conditions, the identity of the customer country, its relationship with the selling country, and the extent of domestic government subsidies. Table 2.3 shows the "cut-rate" prices charged for Russian military equipment in 1993; indeed in an effort to compete commercially and gain hard currency, Moscow was even offering cash customers a ten-year warranty on the latest surface-to-air missiles. Originally having tried to charge much more, the Russians slashed prices to compete with Western suppliers, going from $40 million to $16 million per MiG-27 fighter, for example.[16]

In today's increasingly competitive international arms market, generally referred to as a **buyer's market,** many arms firms now link up across borders, either through takeovers and mergers or through "strategic" corporate alliances, to co-produce or co-market weapons and hence to pool their productive resources and increase sales. Forms of cross-border military corporate collaboration include foreign investment, international subcontracting, international licensing, and joint ventures. If the regulations of one country forbid arms sales to a certain customer, it may still be possible to close a deal by using a foreign partner firm operating under a different set of national regulations and with different market connections. This trend has been referred to as "the internationalization of the arms industry" (see Box 2.2) and is especially prevalent in Europe, where an integrated defense and security community is anticipated by some in the European Community (EC).[17]

BOX 2.2 The Internationalization of Euro-Arms Industries

In parts of the arms industry, but by no means in all sectors, genuine European companies are emerging. ...

In *missile* development and production, the focus is on Euromissile, set up by Aerospatiale and DASA in 1972, and the now emerging collaboration between Matra and BAe [British Aerospace]. ... To compete with their much larger U.S. rivals, such as Martin Marietta or Raytheon, Europe's five largest missile producers may have to merge into one company.

Restructuring is also taking place in the *helicopter* sector. Of the four major West European helicopter producers (Aerospatiale, DASA, Westland and Agusta) two have merged with the establishment of Eurocopter, combining the helicopter branches of Aerospatiale and DASA in a company with 11,950 employees and 11.6 billion French Francs turnover in 1992. According to the chairman of Eurocopter, this merger makes Eurocopter "Europe's largest helicopter manufacturer and the world's largest exporter." He added, however: "The present situation is bad for helicopter manufacturers. ... I think there will be some type of restructuring. People will disappear from the business." As Eurocopter's share of the world military helicopter market has plunged from 20 to 15 per cent in the two years of 1991 and 1992, it could well be that a West European–wide merger is on the agenda.

SOURCE: Elizabeth Sköns and Herbert Wulf, "The Internationalization of the Arms Industry" (Paper presented to the Workshop on Arms Trade and Arms Control in the Post–Cold War World: Future Trends and Developments, Center for War/Peace Studies, Columbia University, New York, November 1993).

Despite the increasingly multinational character of arms production, it still retains a certain power of nationalism. Governments, especially those of major powers, have a deep and abiding interest in controlling or providing for their own forces' armaments and in tracking and regulating the trade in weapons.

Although multinational defense manufacturing collaboration makes sense in forming larger, more competitive units, there is a down side since each separate firm or government has to be satisfied with its role, its revenue, and the control it retains. In the case of jet aircraft production, for example, one producer-country might be assigned the air frame and another the avionics (electronic control systems and radars), while still another is responsible for the engines or attached armaments (missiles, bombs, etc.). Obviously, great care and elaborate planning are necessary to avoid products that resemble camels, "an animal put together by committee." For these reasons, certain projects, such as the next-generation joint British-German-Spanish "Euro-fighter" of the 1990s, have had great difficulty getting off the ground.

Transnational arms production is increasingly seen as a way of sustaining the military-industrial-scientific-technological systems of individual states. The lure of technology sharing and joint arms development competes against each country's own sense of nationalism and fears of competitors getting ahead and also against the reality that international arms production is more expensive than purely national production.[18] Yet the wave of the future appears to favor the larger units and greater market dominance of multinational arms production consortia.[19]

The number of arms-producing companies in any one country depends on the size of the market available to purchase their products. Advanced industrialized countries vary in market size depending upon their own military needs, and such needs are defined by governments and perceived levels of military threat or ambition. Market size ranges from the relatively large demand of U.S. armed forces, at least prior to the defense cuts of the post–cold war era, where it was not unusual to order six hundred or more multimillion-dollar aircraft at a time, to smaller states such as Sweden. Therefore, with less assured markets both larger and smaller states have increasingly been forced to consolidate, or **restructure,** their arms firms through mergers, often by government plan, to support only surviving national "champions." In addition, downsizing has taken place to eliminate what are considered to be excess jobs, often resulting in massive layoffs and unemployment.

Some arms-producing states, such as Russia, still try to retain capacity in all forms of weaponry—land, sea, and air. Others, such as Sweden, increasingly specialize in the type of systems they produce with relative efficiency while importing the remainder of their needs. Even Britain, which traditionally had a very extensive arms-manufacturing sector, retained across-the-board weapon production but also pared down to fewer firms and selective government contract awards; for example, it has concentrated all aircraft and missile production in the British Aerospace Corporation (BAe).

Observers have likened the economic effect of arms production to a narcotic. A supposedly addictive process greatly complicates efforts to control the global spread of weapons or convert from defense to other forms of manufacturing. Arms production takes place in a special type of economic niche, regardless of whether the arms producer has a capitalist, socialist, or fascist government. No matter the form of government, it will have a keen interest in the type, amount, and destination of arms produced within its borders. Therefore, states will be apt both to subsidize such production—even in supposedly free-market economies—and to regulate it. The life's blood of weapons manufacturing—the flow of capital—is likely to be supplemented by government contracts, and the lure of such contracts has tempted many a manufacturing firm and broken many a resolution to convert to civilian products.

Defense spending critics argue that these arrangements, while producing advanced military hardware, are necessarily overly expensive and inefficient in the use of labor. These critics maintain that military and corporate leadership tends to campaign for greater shares of the national budget and influence over the nation's decisionmaking and that more jobs per unit of investment can be generated in the civilian sector, meaning that military production is capital (use of machines and exacting design specifications) rather than labor (mass production employing less skilled workers) intensive. Military production also supposedly is inherently inflationary and subject to cost overruns since governments and armed forces have strong interests in completing projects once they have begun. Even if a weapon system fails to perform up to specifications or expectations, it is very difficult, though not impossible, simply to ditch it once large investments have been made. Yet the goods themselves cannot easily be consumed except in war or military action, so more money chases relatively few goods produced by comparatively few workers.[20]

Reduced defense expenditures do not, however, necessarily lead to immediate economic improvements. Certain groups may benefit from such moves, while others suffer. For example, when the United States demobilized its forces after World War II, many workers and soldiers found jobs in an expanding consumer goods industry, spurred on by pent-up consumer demand after four years of war. But the burden of reduced defense employment was borne primarily by women and minorities, who lost out as "the boys came marching home" to take back their jobs. Government decisions, then, about what to do with peace dividends, whether to invest them in new plants and facilities, whether to encourage savings or consumption, will have much to say about the resulting economic benefits.[21]

The other complication is that separating civilian and military technology is not entirely possible. Electronics are just one example of industries whose breakthroughs aid in both consumer and defense production. Chemicals can be used for both insecticides and nerve gas; synthetic materials, such as epoxies and polymers, the light components of today's aircraft wings, can be part of either fighter planes or passenger jets. Indeed, the United States' greatest military production success, its "arsenal of democracy" in World War II, was Detroit, its motor capital. It is similarly no accident that Brazil got started marketing light armored fighting vehicles in the 1970s after first developing a transplanted automotive industry via Volkswagen.

Arms, then, are both unique and ordinary as part of international trade and commerce. They are unique in their lethality, in their potential to inflict damage on political and human interests. They are familiar in that they are simply goods and services (such as the training or base construction that goes with arms); as with other commercial products, their value is determined by supply and demand and conditioned by subsidy. Thus, in international relations weapons are both an instrument of power and an object of wealth.[22]

BUREAUCRACIES AND ARMS DEVELOPMENT

In Chapter 1 we saw that momentum for rapid change in the development of new arms was built into the international system after the Renaissance and Industrial Revolution. But a brake was put on the process as well. Governments and military officials had an interest in modernizing their weapons arsenals and supported designers, engineers, and manufacturers where possible to do that. Yet inherent in the modern political world was the emergence of bureaucracies (agencies) staffed by specialists and designed to address and solve specific problems (such as building roads or preparing for the common defense).

Bureaucracies develop routines of operation, called **standard operating procedures (SOPS),** that institutionalize memory about how tasks should be done, thereby avoiding the need to "reinvent the wheel" every time a new person comes into the organization. Military SOPS are essentially manuals detailing how to organize efforts ranging from deployment of forces on the battlefield to weapons production contracting. Such procedures are by nature rather inflexible and static over time. They conserve past practice. So in the midst of the great push for weapons innovation beginning in the fourteenth century, there also was a built-in conservatism about how and when to introduce or use new techniques.

Part of this conservatism also resided in the political interests that emerged to keep bureaucracies and organizations going, that is, to compete for budgetary allocations and avoid elimination of jobs. Such bureaucratic politics, noted by a number of social scientists, including Graham Allison (who subsequently served in the Clinton administration Pentagon bureaucracy), both perpetuated the status quo and introduced change at key moments.[23] Therefore, rather than serving a general national interest, weapons innovations, or the delay of innovation, also often served subnational (interest group) or bureaucratic agency interests.

These tendencies are evident in numerous historical examples, ranging from the horse cavalry's stay well beyond its time into the twentieth century to the development of nuclear forces.[24] We need only remember the gallant but appalling scenes of Polish cavalry fighting German tanks in 1939 to appreciate how various countries' military preparations can go "out of kilter" as a result of political and bureaucratic decisionmaking, technological gaps, and budgetary resource allocations. Bureaucratic conservatism and vested interests regarding weaponry are strongly reflected in various nations' military spending patterns. Even though competition among rival states and security threats condition such spending, studies have shown a very strong "inertial" factor as well—the tendency for this year's military budget to reflect last year's.[25] In addition, arms import patterns also tend to be inertial and repetitive; the largest importers during the 1970s also tended to be the largest importers during the 1980s.[26]

However, whether or not government agencies want much change or innovation at any particular time, science tends to march on, especially given continued funding for research labs. As the rate of scientific innovation has picked up over time, weapon developments often have outpaced the political and military doctrines or rationale supposedly controlling them. In democratic theory, the military is supposed to be controlled by civilian leaders, and war is supposed to be only another form of political competition for limited achievable goals—not an exercise in wanton or total destruction and conquest or unlimited vengeance.[27] Yet with the invention of capabilities for ever-greater destruction have come greater difficulties in keeping them and their spread under proper political control.

Ideas for new arms and related technology nearly always originate among civilian designers, engineers, scientists, and inventors. This was true of equipment ranging from eighteenth- and nineteenth-century rifles to twentieth-century planes, tanks, radar, helicopters, and bombs (including nuclear). Yet to bring these ideas to fruition as weapons, the military and other government agencies provide a concentrated dose of funding as well as engineering and political organization and clout. Military officials often serve on staffs considering what new weapons to purchase and can organize teams able to adapt systems to battle needs; former military officials also enter arms-manufacturing firms through what has come to be termed the "revolving door" of job recruitment.[28]

Some of history's most monumental arms innovations have been by massive government projects. The Manhattan Project, the U.S.-U.K. crash program to develop nuclear weapons during World War II before Nazi Germany could do so, was perhaps the greatest of such efforts. In absolute secrecy, top atomic scientists from around the country and abroad were recruited for an intensive research and development effort in the New Mexico mountains. An entire city was established at Los Alamos to house the young and energetic research staff, and vast nuclear fuel research and production sites were located in Tennessee and Washington state. The mission was an unlikely marriage between the U.S. Army, represented by technocratic organizer General Leslie R. Groves, and civilian intellectuals under the brilliant and charismatic nuclear physicist Robert Oppen-heimer. The pursuit of scientific breakthroughs took them on an adventure of discovery leading ultimately to the world's most destructive weapon. At Los Alamos they went ahead and detonated the first fission bomb even after bets had been taken on its potential for igniting the entire earth atmosphere.[29]

Once built and deployed, weapons themselves generally are carefully controlled (kept under close lock and key) by military and political leaders. When political authority breaks down, however, as it did at the end of the cold war in Eastern and Central Europe, a scramble can ensue to pick up equipment from government armories and from the battlefield. In patterns seen from ancient China to contemporary Somalia, the armed militia of competing warlords or clans contend for control of territory as a central government crumbles. Under normal conditions, however, the problems of political control have more to do with weapon developments, deployments, and transfers than with theft or unauthorized access.

THE SECURITY AND WELFARE IMPERATIVES

We have seen, then, that there are two aspects to the arms business: power (relating to security calculations) and wealth (relating to profits and employment, which together promote the welfare of a nation). Indeed, political leaders harbor interests in promoting both security and welfare for their population—defense of borders through military power and improved living conditions (jobs, profits, etc.) within borders through economic and technological development. Arms manufacturing and trade have spread during this century because armament is considered, correctly or not, one way to achieve both security and welfare at the same time.

However, the ability of any single government to promote security and welfare seems increasingly limited by pressures from the domestic and international environments. These pressures include domestic and international security threats from hostile neighbors or dissident ethnic groups as well as the pressures of global economic and environmental trends, such as recession, resource scarcities, pollution, and the need to employ masses of workers in consumer goods production.[30] Also, the technology needed for weapons can seldom be found completely in one place or country; even U.S. leaders felt compelled to include British and German scientists in the Manhattan Project because scientific research tends to be multinational.

We have seen that governments are often very interested in seeing arms manufacturers stay in business. In addition to concern about employment and technological advances, if war should break out political leaders want to maintain the independence their country gains by producing its own weapons rather than depending on possibly uncertain foreign supplies. Military self-reliance supposedly makes the state less vulnerable to foreign interference and manipulation. An added link between employment and security concerns is the danger that well-educated but unemployed engineers and scientists can act as strong vocal opponents of the government at home or can offer their services for sale to potential enemies abroad. Thus, governments ranging from LDCs such as Malaysia to major powers such as Russia have continued to subsidize the weapons business despite budget difficulties.

However, arms autonomy comes at a high price. It is one thing to be able to produce foreign-designed equipment under license, but it is far more difficult to design and produce equipment at even relatively moderate levels of sophistication. Heavy investments are required in fields such as electronics, chemicals, computing, and engineering. Increasing numbers of countries can afford advances in some of these fields, but few can support the full array of capabilities necessary for autonomy. For example, though Israel produces and adapts much of its own equipment, it still relies on outside sources, particularly the United States, for sophisticated key components and technology—such as jet engines. This dependence gives Washington added say in where Israel can sell or use the equipment containing those engines. Israel in turn seeks joint ventures with U.S. firms to gain experience developing such advanced systems as **antiballistic missiles** capable of knocking down incoming missiles carrying highly destructive **warheads** (bombs).

The security and welfare motives involved in arms manufacturing, joint ventures, and trade produce great cross-pressures on governments. On the one hand, international security policy, which often involves threats and counterthreats, can degenerate into persistent conflicts, and each weapons-manufacturing country will seek to guard its secrets. On the other hand, international economic marketing, while involving competition, can generate (at least in theory) mutually beneficial exchanges that do not create permanent enemies. In the process, however, potentially dangerous technologies and industrial secrets might have to be shared. U.S. and Japanese firms and government agencies have discussed joint defense and aerospace technology sharing, but each side has also worried that the other would gain technological advantage from such collaboration.

Mixed motives and security tension were also evident in the multiple arms sales to Iran and Iraq during their long war of the 1980s. Companies could profit and governments supposedly could keep both Iran and Iraq from winning a decisive victory in the oil-rich Gulf through such supplies. Washington even violated its own arms embargo to the region, "Operation Staunch," when tempted to sell arms for political and economic gain (see Box 1.1 in Chapter 1). The ultimate overarming of Iraq, resulting from sales by some two dozen suppliers, had repercussions in Iraq's attack on Kuwait in 1990 and showed that such overambitious arms policies, when left unchecked, could be disastrous.

The type of security policy a state adopts will condition the type of armament it requires. For example, a strategy premised on **forward defense**—defending allies distant from a country's shores or borders rather than waiting for a homeland attack—-will require more naval, long-range aircraft and transport capability. A state relying on **continental defense,** as Australia did in the 1980s, forgoes the quest for overseas bases and concentrates on defending the homeland. This defensive posture can require large reserve forces and the ability to patrol borders very efficiently in fast attack craft, planes, helicopters, and vehicles.

By the same token, if a state wishes to produce its own arms, especially sophisticated arms, it may have to adjust its defense-related requirements to market conditions. This state must produce weapons that it can use but that also appeal to potential foreign buyers in order to sustain the level of production needed to bring costs down. Thus, pure military priorities give way to commercial concerns, and purely domestic arms production gives way to the global arms market. The armed services sometimes are forced to accept marketable weapons they do not really want; top-of-the-line equipment can be sold to foreign buyers before the home troops even have access to it (both of which have happened to the French army at various times, including advanced arms sales to Iraq in the 1980s).

The quest for security produces the armament adequacy dilemma mentioned in the Introduction. The more one state acquires arms or allies to defend itself from foreign threat, for example, the more foreign opponents feel threatened and seek arms or allies of their own.[31] Thus, despite great financial cost in weapon acquisitions, neither side feels more secure; yet they tend to go on in self-reinforcing and expensive arms races, at least partly from fear of losing out to some opponent's new weapons breakthrough. Such races occur not just among major powers but also between traditional regional opponents such as Israel and Syria or India and Pakistan. On the welfare side, arms races tend to perpetuate jobs in the defense sector and also to reflect cultural or ideological commitment as well as fears of foreign enemies.

If we explore the lure of military technology, we also come upon the dilemma of alternatives. If it is true that civilian technology sectors tend to employ more workers, produce more consumer-relevant products, and better equip a state for international trade (consider Japan's success), then too much reliance on the military sector can erode the economy it supposedly benefits. Indeed, too much military spending in a weak consumer

Arms races and the "bottom line." Kirk/The Toledo Blade, OH/Rothco.

economy can fatally cripple economic development, a fact that seemed to characterize the downfall of the Soviet Union.[32] Thus, as implied by the political dilemma of arms acquisition, even the security of the state can be imperiled by equipment meant to protect it—either in the hands of rebels against the government, in an overtaxing of the economy, or both.

As states try to extricate themselves from the arms overdependence and overspending dilemmas, they also suffer short-term dislocations of unemployment and sagging exports. The temptation to keep selling arms and satisfying at least part of the country—a form of short-term political insurance—can be irresistible.

THE RISE OF NEW ARMS PRODUCERS

These conflicting dilemmas can be seen quite clearly in the case of some notable Third World arms producers and exporters. Such states reacted to security and welfare pressures to produce arms but added an additional intense desire to catch up with the world leaders in technology. Brazil, for example, faced with no immediate security threat on its borders, nevertheless emerged during the 1970s among the leaders in Third World arms production (see Box 2.3). Some might therefore conclude that this status was due solely to commercial trade motives. But they neglect the way governments have come to view technology as a key to security. National leaders now see real or imagined threats posed by the **international**

BOX 2.3 The History of Brazil's EMBRAER Aircraft Industry

Brazilian leaders launched EMBRAER in the 1970s despite discouraging economic estimates given the highly competitive international aerospace market, which was dominated by the United States and Europe. EMBRAER was not expected to make a profit but rather to set the stage for Brazil's entry into advanced technologies of all sorts. Cooperation with foreign firms (especially U.S. and Italian) to gain access to the latest aerospace technologies was part of the plan; engineers were to seek projects that promised valuable "spinoffs" for Brazil's aircraft industry and economy in general.

Several successful aircraft, from civilian to military transports to trainers and small fighters, resulted. Brazil tried to customize its products for particular customer needs neglected by larger producers, whose designs were mainly for their own military specifications. Thus, the entire range of motives from commercial to technological to military played a role, but the overall thrust, particularly through technological development, was to propel Brazil onto the stage as a significant power.

SOURCE: Renato Dagnino and Domicio Proenca, Jr., "Arms Production and Technological Spinoffs: The Brazilian Aeronautics Industry" (1989, mimeographed), p. 8.

power structure (the regional or global distribution of capabilities and resources) in general. They do not want to be caught short on general capabilities even if a specific enemy cannot be defined; they wish to keep pace technologically and militarily with other powers, while harnessing their nation's economy to the task.[33]

That such leaders may be misguided misses the point; their image of what is best for themselves and their states is what drives them. Coming late to the arms-exporting game, however, new arms-producing states such as Brazil have proven highly vulnerable to economic and market downturns.

With technological needs and threat perception as guides, we can highlight the similarities and differences in armament patterns of other rising powers such as India and China. India, for example, has generally followed a policy of purchasing high-quality foreign weapons while energetically developing its own domestic products as well. Indeed, the Indian Defence Ministry has announced plans to increase exports of India's own arms products, developed in part to reduce foreign dependency, in order to pay for desired weapon imports.[34] Thus, Indian forces so far appear to have preferred foreign arms designs to their own domestic ones; because of low cost and easy availability, these foreign imports often came from the Soviet Union during the cold war, but a sprinkling of French, British, and U.S. equipment was coveted as well. China, by contrast, apparently has sought to import foreign weapons mainly in order to better perfect its own domestic designs, which it then reexports.[35]

Such differences may be due partly to historic and strategic considerations, such as India's pressing ethnic and border conflicts with both Pakistan and China and the leftover, postcolonial desire of India's forces for prestigious foreign equipment. India also was occasionally boycotted by foreign arms suppliers (the United Kingdom and the United States) in the 1960s and 1970s, when its wartime policies were not satisfactory to those suppliers, but continued to have broad access to Soviet arms. China, however, endured more lean years of foreign arms boycott, both Soviet and Western, and had to develop more revolutionary self-reliance for weaponry. Chinese forces also found themselves with quite outmoded military hardware in comparison to the major powers (the United States and USSR) and even to smaller neighbors (Vietnam and India) with which they competed in the 1970s and 1980s. Therefore, with global security needs and a relatively limited industrial base, China tried to play a quick game of catchup in the arms race.

Both India and China retain apparent ambitions to be regionally influential and even dominant powers, and states such as Brazil and Argentina sometimes are suspected of such ambitions as well. For such states' leaders and armed forces, weapons are insurance against an uncertain future. Whether or not an immediate domestic or foreign security threat exists, in the long run one may emerge. For better or worse, then, although economic productivity is the emerging key to world power, the defining characteristic of great power status is still thought to be the mix and types of weapons a state possesses; they seem to be tickets to the great power table. In the process, selling weapons off to others as well can be both economically necessary and profitable.

As governments increase their militarization, they may do so either through acquisition of advanced weaponry or through reliance on the size of fighting forces (numbers of personnel). These forms of defense have been termed capital intensive and labor intensive, respectively. States also can seek high levels of military self-reliance or content themselves with dependence on foreign arms suppliers and advisers. As a rule of thumb, most militarization in today's world can be classified as capital intensive and dependent.[36] A few states, notably China, Pakistan, India, and Iran, have combined a quest for high-technology arms with reliance on large masses of troops, though China also made significant troop cuts as border tensions eased and as weapons modernization was stressed in the late 1980s.

The predominant capital-intensive/dependent condition means that there is much potential for a continual global arms trade but also that defense strategies relying on high technology become very costly very quickly. Only a relatively few states can afford the latest or high-technology armament, though various lower-priced imitations and guided missiles are finding their way onto the market. One other irony of arms production is evident as well: For major power and minor power military leaders alike, arms have become both a symbol of advanced technological status and a reason to be wary of warfare. Costly investments in producing or purchasing advanced equipment can mean a reluctance to risk losing it in war, especially against difficult opponents and without guaranteed resupply. Thus, in recent wars some leaders—such as Iraq's Hussein facing U.S. forces in 1991 or Argentina's generals facing Britain in the Falkland/Malvinas Islands in 1982—chose not to employ their best, most advanced arms, at least partly for fear of heavy losses. In fact, Iraq sent most of its latest fighter aircraft to its recent enemy, Iran, for "safekeeping" rather than commit them to battle with the latest U.S. jets.

CONCLUSION

We are left, then, with a curious mixture of power and economic games in the arms business, in which technology plays a pivotal role; a global hierarchy of arms developers and suppliers ranges from the very advanced to the relatively primitive. Several questions remain for debate and research:

☐ Can there be strong global or regional powers without heavy reliance on the military and military production?

☐ Is technology itself a false and dehumanizing god that concentrates too much power in the hands of a techno-elite producing and selling advanced weapons and pays too few economic and social dividends?

☐ Does the god of military high technology actually drain the economies of less developed states, leading them to specialize in expensively produced products for which the long-term market prospect is poor?

☐ Does overemphasis on military production erode the economies and trade competitiveness of major powers as well?

☐ Should states in need of defense, including the United States, rely more on foreign weapons, trading off autonomy for cost savings?

☐ Would some states be better off with nonmilitary defense strategies, such as civilian-based resistance, passive resistance, or reliance on allies or international organizations for protection?

☐ Is there a solution to the alternatives dilemma that would allow for large-scale conversion from defense to civilian goods production without politically unacceptable unemployment levels?

If states pin their hopes for great power status exclusively on weapons, they may be disappointed. The weapons market, as we have seen, is subject to notorious ups and downs. Furthermore, autonomy and even security as strategic or technological ideals have proven elusive. States rely increasingly on foreign partnership to get ahead technologically; even U.S. manufacturers, with their relative dominance of the weapons market, are pursuing numerous joint international ventures for various benefits of technology, shared markets, cheaper labor, and investment capital. Arms firms along with other industries have entered a period of restructuring, sometimes downsizing, sometimes expanding by merger, sometimes dropping defense production, sometimes dropping civilian production to concentrate on defense, or sometimes combining the two in dual use products. Diverse strategies are being adopted in a sea of international competition with relatively restricted government funding.

The questions just raised concern the ultimate viability of the "defense economy." Ultimately they must be answered by citizens and by individual governments and firms mapping their own arms spending and manufacturing moves. Clearly, however, the defense economy is the driving force behind the global arms trade, the means and motives for which are more thoroughly explored in the next chapter.

THREE

□ □ □

Arms Transfers and
World Politics

I n an interview with a prominent Egyptian journalist shortly after the
destructive 1973 Arab-Israeli War, Secretary of State Henry Kissinger
explained Washington's decision finally to resupply the hard-pressed Israelis with arms after prior delays by saying, "Do not deceive yourself, the
United States could not—either today or tomorrow—allow Soviet arms to
win a big victory, even if it was not decisive, against U.S. arms. This has
nothing to do with Israel or with you."[1] This remarkable statement shows
that during the cold war superpower leaders were at least as worried
about the reputation of their weapons in battle as about the survival of
their regional clients and friends. The Nixon administration had delayed
resupply evidently in hopes of pressuring Israel toward a negotiated settlement but quickly reversed course when the Israelis seemed in danger of
being overwhelmed, with resultant embarrassment for Washington.
Arms had become a key to superpower status and influence, or at least
supposed influence, to persuade or dissuade friends and foes.

Much is revealed here about the reasons for the arms manufacturing
and proliferation patterns seen in Chapters 1 and 2. Recall that weapons
are developed and distributed by states and firms for a mixture of economic and strategic reasons. Economics entails employment and longer
production runs at the factory as well as commercial trading, industrial
manufacturing, and technological development motives. Strategy entails
an array of goals, including (1) homeland defense and the myth of autonomy and self-sufficiency; (2) desires to show the benefits of associating
with the arms-supplying state—that is, "better" weapons can be obtained
from this state than from its rivals; (3) bolstering of favored clients to promote regional power balances, which can mean having to prevent the fall
or defeat of those clients; and (4) maneuvering of recipient states to adopt
policies preferred by the arms supplier—that is, bargaining through arms

supply to obtain concessions such as military base rights or votes in the United Nations.

A key distinction in the arms trade is between suppliers interested mainly in strategic considerations—primarily the United States and, while it existed, the USSR—and those in the business mainly for commercial interests (European and NIC suppliers).[2] Strategic suppliers seek to manipulate regional power balances and maintain favorable access and outcomes abroad by using arms supplies as a form of reward or punishment. Secretary Kissinger was playing such a role with Israel in 1973, and the long-term reputation of the arms being supplied was quite important to him in maintaining advantages in this game. Strategic suppliers presumably would draw the line at transferring arms to unfriendly or potentially dangerous regimes.

Research has shown, however, that arms transfers are a relatively unreliable form of political and strategic influence; although they can sustain a client in a fight or war, they seldom extract major political concessions or reforms from such clients.[3] Transfers seem more effective in winning immediate short-term concessions, such as base rights, than in building the donor's overall long-term influence over the recipient's policies or remaking regional arms balances. Even short-term concessions may be winnable in only a portion of cases; one study has concluded around 50 percent of the time.[4]

Commercial suppliers care less about such influence and concentrate instead on the revenues or jobs generated by arms exports. Presumably they also care less about the identity or political allegiance of the recipient and more about its credit ratings and ability to pay. They may even supply arms to both sides of a war (strategic suppliers also might do so if a stalemate was the desired outcome). Here too there is interest in the reputation of weapons for superior quality as compared to those of opponents, but the interest is primarily in long-term sales prospects rather than political influence.

For many arms suppliers, and even the superpowers at various moments, these interests obviously are mixed, especially when concerns about technology are considered. Britain, Germany, and France, for example, with limited domestic arms markets because of relatively small military services, promote foreign exports in order to keep their arms industries going. We have seen such industries are considered strategically important to the nation's future defense, and thus strategy mixes with economic gain to dictate the marketing of arms. Germany and Japan, however, because of past military excesses, have constitutions that limit both their military activities abroad and their military exports to war-ridden regions. Joining in multinational weapon-production and marketing consortia has been one way for them to obscure the extent of their military marketing and partially avoid the merchants of death label.

In theory, strategic suppliers such as the United States are expected to be more manipulative about arms transfers than commercial suppliers; we would expect more arms embargoes and supply slowdowns or restrictions from strategically motivated states. However, nearly all arms-supplying states employ some restrictions on exports. Even while pushing to develop commercial weapons sales in the 1990s, for example, Russia has maintained and supported U.N. arms embargoes of Iraq and the former Yugoslavia (despite political interests on the Serbian side). States employ arms export regulations and limitations generally to keep better track of their weapons and related technological secrets, with some care as to where and in whose hands they end up. At the very least, military commanders do not relish the prospect of having to fight against their own equipment in the hands of foreign armies or terrorist groups. When Afghani rebels reportedly dished off advanced U.S. "Stinger" mobile anti-aircraft missiles to their Iranian neighbors in the late 1980s, however, it became apparent that ultimate **end use** controls on where weapons exports end up may be deficient even for strategic suppliers.

The prestige of acquiring the "best" arms has a certain market appeal; states presumably will not as readily challenge forces equipped with the most devastating weapons. Arms supply has many ethical dilemmas, however, as equipment in some sense becomes more important than people or property. For example, arms-supplying states have been accused of using regions such as the Middle East and Southeast Asia as battlefield proving grounds for the latest technologies (anti-aircraft, antitank, stealth, smart bombs, etc.), with little regard to the death tolls inflicted.

TO SELL OR NOT TO SELL?

The impulse to export arms, either for profit or to "win friends and influence people," often runs squarely up against states' other interests in keeping lethal equipment from the "wrong people." We saw in Chapter 2 that arms manufacturers historically have been both nurtured and restrained by governments since they fill the dual role of needed supplier of a state's own forces and feared supplier of enemies. This tension and dilemma of arms transfers remain unresolved and indeed grow more complicated with the trend toward exports not only of weapons but also of weapon-related components, dual use equipment, know-how, and technology. Some countries have even devised weapons specifically for export, often keeping them a step below the latest designs; but such equipment may not satisfy the demand of the most ambitious customers for top-of-the-line equipment. Therefore, weapons-related exports seem to generate ever-more controversies, and it is increasingly difficult to know what is or is not an "arms transfer."

In governments of major arms-supplying states, review agencies in the departments or ministries of defense, commerce, treasury, intelligence, and foreign affairs often meet on controversial cases to consider the worthiness of a prospective arms recipient. Their criteria can range from the stability and friendliness of the client government to its likely involvement in war, creditworthiness, and ability to pay, along with possible effects on neighboring states and prevailing opinion in world organizations such as the United Nations.

Recently this concern has been heightened by the global spread of more sophisticated armament. Thus, groups of major powers have sought to track, coordinate, or limit weapon and technology supplies to conflict-prone regions such as the Middle East. Most such efforts falter once the temptation for major arms deals becomes irresistible.

Furthermore, agencies making arms transfer decisions often have conflicting priorities about specific deals. Foreign ministries and diplomats, especially in major powers, generally have favored selling or transferring arms as a way to cement relations with favored foreign governments; the argument "If our country doesn't sell it to them, some other country will" is often repeated. One assumes that arms sales at least afford the seller some degree of influence over the recipient; in early U.S. weapon sales to Pakistan, for example, the number of spare parts was strictly limited to keep a sort of leash on that state's war-fighting possibilities vis-à-vis India. The same was true of some Soviet Middle Eastern shipments.[5] Diplomats will sometimes call for halts and embargoes of arms deliveries to pressure or penalize states or to conform to the desires of other friendly governments and organizations.

Despite a sometimes militarist image, defense ministries and military staff frequently oppose specific weapon transfers and sales, fearing the release of the most advanced arms technologies and resenting the drain on government arsenals in order to supply foreigners. Yet some in defense agencies also favor exports as a way of keeping the price down and production capability up for new equipment and as a way of regaining research and development funds.

Restrictions on arms transfers vary in comprehensiveness and enforcement, and range from the end use statements required by Washington, whereby final destinations must be designated and unauthorized use or reexport of arms to other countries is formally prohibited, to the **areas-of-crisis regulations** employed by Germany, which prohibit the export of arms to unstable and conflict-prone regions. In recent years the United States has added a twist to such areas-of-crisis criteria by promising not to introduce newer higher levels of arms technology to regions not yet possessing them.

Unfortunately, however, predictions of "good" weapons sale risks—for example, those states that would use arms only if attacked and would safeguard them from being used against the interest of the supplier—are seldom easy or highly accurate. Furthermore, effective enforcement of final destination clauses can be quite difficult and could require aborting the donor state's relations with the recipient. Finally, it is difficult to obtain unanimity among all supplying states on provisions such as areas-of-crisis or level-of-technology restrictions.

The dilemma of promoting and attempting to restrict sales at the same time is evident in some recent U.S. policies. As a strategically minded exporter, Washington has been quite sensitive to other states' acquisition of ballistic missiles and nuclear technology, which could threaten U.S. allies or U.S. territory itself. Thus, it has promoted the **Missile Technology Control Regime (MTCR),** which is a set of international agreements among exporters to restrain the supply of missiles to dangerous regions. The State Department has been very critical of North Korea for selling such equipment to Syria, for example, and has called for sanctions denying contracts and arms exports to North Korea by way of retaliation. North Korea's relative isolation from many major powers and Western allies ironically has made that state more immune to such pressures. Also, late in 1992 Washington moved, with some European support, to tighten multilateral limits on weapon sales to Iran, though the commercial interests of suppliers such as China and Russia make them uncertain partners in these efforts.

There are many exceptions to such limits, even for the United States, one of their chief proponents. The Pressler amendment of 1990 to the Foreign Assistance Act, for example, provided that U.S. assistance and military equipment should be denied to Pakistan if the president cannot certify that Pakistani forces do not possess a nuclear explosive device. However, when the amendment took effect, although President George Bush could no longer provide this certification, the State Department nevertheless approved more than $120 million in commercial arms sales to Pakistan, arguing that such nongovernment sales were not covered in the ban. Pakistan was still seen as an important strategic ally. Going further in the midst of a reelection battle in 1992, the Bush administration, worried about defense industry unemployment in key states such as Missouri, authorized the controversial sale of the McDonnell-Douglas F-15 combat aircraft to Saudi Arabia. Requirements that exporting companies repay government research and development subsidies were also removed.[6] Thus, despite its efforts to convince other countries to restrain their weapons shipments, Washington went ahead with record levels of its own arms transfers.

The United States has not been the only state criticized for lax arms export controls. Illegal German and Swedish arms and equipment shipments to customers such as Iraq and India were uncovered in the 1980s and 1990s, causing scandals and even playing a part in the downfall of governments. Tensions between the sales impulse and security worries require careful policies aimed at providing alternate ways to advance commerce and reduce threats of military attack at the same time.

Washington, Moscow, Paris, London, and other major powers at least have been able to agree relatively firmly on the necessity of limiting the spread of nuclear weapons and weapons of mass destruction (chemical and biological) and thus promoting greater stability and predictability in international relations. When a suspicious flash, possibly indicating a nuclear test, was recorded by a Soviet satellite off the coast of South Africa in the late 1970s, despite the cold war it was first reported to Washington, and joint investigations immediately commenced. Yet even though international organizations, such as the consultative **Nuclear Suppliers Group** and the inspecting and standard-setting **International Atomic Energy Agency (IAEA),** exist to regulate the spread of nuclear weapons components and fuels, they have not always been given the strongest U.S. backing or staff support to carry on their functions. South Africa later admitted that it had indeed manufactured nuclear weapons and that the international community had done little about it.[7]

The entire structure of the Nuclear Non-proliferation Treaty of 1970, ratified by more than 140 countries, is based on multilateral cooperation and on a political consensus between nuclear and non-nuclear states to allow nuclear energy to be available for peaceful purposes (in medicine and for electricity, etc.) but to restrict the nuclear arsenals of the great powers and keep smaller powers from ever acquiring such weapons. Indeed, the NPT, which comes up for renewal in the mid-1990s, is often cited as a model for possible conventional weapon controls since it includes both penalties for noncooperation and incentives for cooperation to restrict access to weapons. However, to retain broad international support, such agreements simultaneously have to provide their members with security and access to new technologies.

As seen in Box 3.1, the difficulties of these control efforts are extensive and involve direct bilateral and third-party relations. These difficulties relate to the access, adequacy, and alternatives dilemmas in that some countries are assuming the role of telling others what they should or should not develop, export, or import. Does any single state or group of states have the authority to regulate arms reaching certain volatile regions in a sovereign state system? Some in the developing world would argue, for

BOX 3.1 Resolving an Arms Transfer Dispute

Under pressure from the United States, Russia agreed [in July 1993] to halt its planned sale of equipment and technology to India that U.S. experts said could be used to make a ballistic missile. ...

In a compromise that ended a bitter year-long dispute, the United States won Russian approval for the halt of the sale in return for waiving economic sanctions that had been set to go into effect ... against two Russian companies involved in the deal.

In addition, the agreement held out the prospect of potentially lucrative joint space projects. ...

The dispute over the missile was the most serious disagreement between Russia and the United States on security issues since the fall of the Soviet Union in 1991. It also provided the Clinton Administration with the first serious test of its policy of seeking to penalize countries that spread technology for nuclear, chemical and bacteriological weapons and ballistic missiles. ...

Moscow had urged that it must be able to sell its military hardware and expertise around the world in order to earn hard currency. ...

Russia agreed to halt the transfer of sophisticated rocket engines and related technology to India under a contract that dates back to the Soviet era. ... Even more important in the long term, Russia agreed to adhere to terms of the Missile Technology Control Regime. ...

Some Administration nonproliferation experts complained that the compromise may be meaningless, because they believe that Russia has already shipped much of the technology that India needs and New Delhi could get whatever technology it would still need from another source, possibly China.

Other experts praised the agreement, but noted that it does not address the larger issue of Russia's other military sales around the world. ...

"The agreement is significant because it bolsters the Missile Technology Control Regime and will give Russia's aerospace engineers something to do in Russia rather than in ... North Korea. ..."

The agreement is likely to worsen U.S. relations with India, [however,] which argued that it wanted to use the Russian-designed rocket engine to enter the commercial satellite-launching industry. ...

The United States, however, fears that India's rocket-launching capabilities could lead to a missile race on the subcontinent, where tensions are already high because of the weapons buildup and nuclear programs of India and Pakistan.

SOURCE: Elaine Sciolino, "Russia Is Halting Arms-Linked Sales," *New York Times,* July 17, 1993. Copyright © 1993 by The New York Times Company. Reprinted by permission.

example, that if North America, Europe, Russia, China, Israel, and South Asia all have nuclear weapons and delivery systems, why should Africa, Latin America, Iraq, Iran, or North Korea be left out of this "defense" league? Major weapons, after all, can represent a ticket to the bargaining table for important negotiations about such issues as disarmament, arms control, or regional political settlements. In Chapter 4 the possibilities and complications of multinational arms control decisions and **regimes** (networks of international regulatory agencies) are explored.

THE BLACK AND GRAY ARMS MARKETS

We saw in Chapter 2 that not all arms transfers proceed through government or even legitimate industry channels. Arms also are a lucrative business for smugglers, terrorists, and a variety of other interest groups, including covert government agencies engaging in secret deliveries. The illegal, or covert, side of the arms trade has received increased attention in recent years, primarily because it has come to involve larger shipments of more potent weapons: "advanced helicopters, entire jet combat aircraft and components, ... missiles and cluster bombs." This illicit trade has existed to a certain extent for centuries but generally had involved only small arms. Estimates now put this trade at about $5–10 billion per year.[8]

Analysts have broken such sales down into what might be called gray and black markets. The former refers to governmentally approved or covert arms shipments that skirt the letter of the law or evade international restrictions and embargoes, such as U.S. government assistance to the Nicaraguan contra and Afghan mujahideen rebels fighting Marxist governments in the 1980s. In some of those deals, U.S. agencies raised private monies or dealt with shady third parties to finance and arrange the arms shipments. Sometimes secret permission also is granted to transship equipment across the territory of other countries.

The black market involves unlawful or unapproved transfers by private arms dealers and smugglers. Usually these are smaller arms because of the difficulty of packaging and concealing major weapons transfers without some government cooperation. Because of shifting regulatory legislation and the growth of the weapons component and technology trade, it appears that the black market, which historically has been a reaction to and way around embargoes, is giving way little by little to the gray. The gray market grows when government officials at least "look the other way" as their agencies arrange for arms to be sent to foreign groups and countries for profit, strategic calculation, or both.[9]

Interestingly, arms transferred under such illicit or semi-illicit deals appear more likely to be used in battle than normal legal government-to-government transfers since pressure for them is likely to stem from imme-

BOX 3.2 The Riddle of Drug Traffickers on the Arms Market

Among sub-national actors, the black market probably is of greatest importance to drug cartels. They have the financial and organizational resources to acquire large scale capabilities through numerous small scale transactions. ... Latin American narcotics traffickers have acquired much of their firepower from unlicensed purchases on the U.S. private gun market. With over 200 million firearms in private hands, the United States has unlimited potential for illegal diversions.

During the 1980s it became common practice for smugglers to buy weapons legally in American shops for illegal resale in Latin America. ... For many years the private American gun market was unique as a source of automatic rifles ideally suited to internal conflict. ... With disintegration of the Soviet Union and collapse of police and military authority, Russia now is in a similar situation. ...

Fears that drug barons would use their funds to systematically arm their own huge private armies have proven to be unfounded. The largest arms sales involving drug marketeers probably are of little use to themselves; they avoid conflict with the state through bribery and intimidation, not organized warfare. The most dangerous adversaries with whom drug dealers must contend are their competitors, and this risk seems to be managed through Mafia-style syndicates. Transactions involving more than a few hundred rifles are more likely to be brokered for third parties, most notably sympathetic insurgents like the Revolutionary Armed Forces of Colombia (FARC) and Peru's Shining Path. ...

[Drug cartels] supplied the U.S. M-60 machine guns, 81mm mortars and grenade launchers that arm the Shining Path's heaviest forces. ...

[But] even drug dealers prefer to buy through licensed exporters. ... Through legal deals they receive better quality equipment at a lower price, and they minimize the risk of prosecution. Cooperation with Western security and intelligence agencies created opportunities for legal arms acquisition in the 1980s. The greed, disregard and poor regulation by established exporters create [other such opportunities].

SOURCE: Aaron Karp, "The Black and Grey Markets" (Paper presented at the Workshop on Arms Trade and Arms Control in the Post–Cold War World: Future Trends and Developments, Center for War/Peace Studies, Columbia University, New York, November 1993), pp. 6–7.

diate war needs. Thus, these deals represent a challenge to government policymaking because they generally occur without full official consideration or public debate and because they increase the chances and severity of further fighting. So-called pariah states, those such as South Africa that have been denied normal arms shipments because of human rights and other abuses, shop and sell heavily in black and gray markets, but others, including terrorist groups, criminals, and legitimate governments, do too (see Box 3.2). States such as Israel, Taiwan, and others, when denied the latest advanced technologies, evidently have tried to smuggle in desired goods. With the end of the cold war, it has been rumored that Russian, Ukrainian, and Chinese military "agencies" have at times acted "on their own" to sell such goods to various customers.[10]

Among the recent conflict zones that have received heavy doses of black and gray arms are

- ☐ Afghanistan (U.S. arms with financing by Saudi Arabia and Arab Gulf states, Egypt, China, and Iran)
- ☐ Angola (U.S. and Soviet arms)
- ☐ Bosnia (supplies via Iran, Lebanon, Europe, the United States)
- ☐ Colombia (smuggling in drug trade)
- ☐ Nicaragua (contra aid from the United States and Israel)
- ☐ Croatia (Bulgarian arms, possible Chilean shipments)
- ☐ Iran (various illegal or illicit shipments from the United States, Germany, Italy, Sweden, France, Austria, Czechoslovakia, Afghanistan, North Korea, and China)
- ☐ Iraq (cluster bombs from Chile and possible nuclear components from Europe)
- ☐ Israel (U.S. nuclear triggering devices smuggled in early 1980s)
- ☐ Kashmir (transfers from Pakistan and Afghanistan)
- ☐ Libya (U.S. and other supplies and spare parts through private channels)
- ☐ Pakistan (nuclear-related equipment from a large network of sources as well as many arms from the Afghan war)
- ☐ South Africa (components from German and U.S. firms).[11]

ARMS TRANSFERS AND CONFLICT

It should now be clear from the preceding review of the roots and growth of global arms proliferation in relation to conflict zones that this proliferation is a major public policy problem. This problem relates to the classic question of whether arms are responsible for killing or are merely an extension of the destructive human psyche, which is itself the real problem. This formulation is what I have termed the causation dilemma. As one prominent private arms dealer maintained in a personal interview, "War is the depth of human folly; I merely plumb the depths." In other words, the customer is responsible for what is done with the arms.

Even though this remark seems a convenient rationalization for someone making healthy profits by distributing war materiel, it is extremely difficult to determine what "causes killing." One way to approach this chicken-and-egg problem is to look at the frequency of war following the buildup of arms or arms races. Indeed, the private dealer just quoted would be reassured to know that most studies fail to show that all arms buildups result in war; one need only look at the general avoidance of mutual armed confrontation by Washington and Moscow during their four-decades-long cold war arms race.

However, an arms buildup by at least one of the parties has preceded nearly all wars during the past two centuries, and during the cold war the Soviet Union and the United States fueled many a war in the Third World.[12] Furthermore, we have seen that private and covert arms sales are especially likely to end up in warfare. In other words, "armament does not, as its opponents think, inevitably lead to war, though it can increase regional instabilities and sharpen existing conflicts."[13]

Generally, states seem to begin wars with a sense of preparedness and optimism, often sustained through arms acquisition.[14] Obviously, wars end if neither side has weapons, parts, or fuel, even if the underlying political conflicts have not been solved. Fighting may recur, however, when the parties see strategic advantages in their own strength or their opponent's weakness.

It is difficult to argue that arms are an unmitigated evil. Who would deny the victims of outright aggression or genocide the right to defend themselves against their oppressors? The U.N. Charter legitimizes the right of individual and collective self-defense, even while outlawing aggressive warfare. During the brief 1969 Central American war (commonly dubbed the "football war" since it began after soccer matches) between two small and impoverished states, Honduras and El Salvador, which involved a dispute over peasant immigrants, Honduras indeed asked the Organization of American States (OAS) to provide it with arms as the victim of aggression, and for a time the OAS held open the possibility of doing so in order to pressure El Salvador into a cease-fire.[15] Similar notions occurred as governments wondered how to stop the bloody carnage in the former Yugoslavia in the early 1990s; Washington debated the wisdom of ending the comprehensive arms embargo by permitting shipments to the beleaguered Bosnian Muslims. It was decided not to do so, however, for fear of escalating the general level of fighting and arms smuggling and of endangering U.N. peacekeeping personnel.

It is difficult to determine who is "at fault" in many wars since no one admits to aggression and most fighters can point to some real or supposed provocation; atrocities are often not confined to one side. Thus, again some would say that the only sure path to peace is to outlaw war or ban arms altogether, for initiator or defender, while others would draw distinctions under international law and allow for defensive (e.g., anti-aircraft missiles) as opposed to offensive (e.g., long-range bombers) arms and fighting.

Of course, any weapon could be used either for defense or offense, depending upon the context, as when anti-aircraft missiles accompany troops as they move forward into the enemy's territory. Late in the cold war, when Soviet tank strength seemed able to overwhelm NATO defenses, the United States took the lead in designing **neutron bombs,** so-called enhanced radiation nuclear weapons that would yield less blast and higher doses of lethal radiation. Washington argued that this would provide safer, more effective defense in the crowded European continent by reducing destruction of cities while focusing radiation on invading Soviet tank crews. Moscow, however, never accepted the argument that these were defensive arms meant to overcome a disadvantage, maintaining that they could also be used to invade the East, sparing towns while killing Soviet defenders in the process.

In view of the dilemmas of self-defense, some would advocate unarmed (passive or active) citizen-based resistance, or civilian-based defense, on the order of Mahatma Gandhi's or Martin Luther King's philosophies.[16] These advocates note that, depending upon the circumstances and the opponent's bloodthirstiness, such resistance can be very effective and can save lives and diminish wasteful arms spending. With the bitter experience of history, however, few appear ready yet to trust unarmed defense unless the enemy is certified to have a conscience.

Therefore, although wars may not always be the direct result, the global spread of weapons has in many ways tended to exacerbate, rather than relieve, the security dilemmas and tensions noted in the Introduction.

> Increased levels of armaments under conditions of the security dilemma lead to an upward spiral of armaments and military spending, the exacerbation of conflicts by worst-case thinking, and a concomitant decline in interstate security. An example of this would be the Latin-U.S. race to acquire supersonic fighters in the 1960s. Peru was the first state to acquire such planes; by 1975 Argentina, Brazil, Chile, and Venezuela had all followed suit. No war broke out, none was intended, and all states were forced to spend more than they would have wanted on national defense.[17]

Besides escalating the cost of defense (it has been estimated that Israel's 1973 war with Egypt and Syria cost Israel the rough equivalent of an entire year's national income), today's capital-intensive militarization often proves poorly suited to actual defense needs. Libya imported up to 1,200 tanks and 450 MiG fighters from the USSR in the 1980s, only to keep them basically in storage, even during its relatively unsuccessful military campaigns in neighboring Chad. Part of Libya's reason for purchasing the equipment had little to do with its own defense needs; some of the equipment was made available to North African neighbors such as Egypt in order to cement Tripoli's political influence and was later returned to Libyan arsenals.[18] High-priced sophisticated weapons, and a lack of skilled personnel to use them, can lead to a "you use it, you lose it" mentality. Perhaps this is good for peace, but it is an odd way of achieving it. Oddly enough, it appears that less advanced arms, such as rifles and artillery, are likely to lead sooner to bloodshed. Furthermore, well-timed doses of certain equipment can be highly effective for defense, as Afghan and Vietnamese rebels showed by employing mobile anti-aircraft missiles effectively to down Soviet and U.S. aircraft during their long struggles.

Arms supplies, or the denial of them, however, appear to be relatively unreliable in controlling or ending wars or conflicts already under way. It has been argued that "increased availability of sophisticated weapons tends to increase the destructiveness of war when it breaks out."[19] Yet we also have seen that well-timed arms shipments, or the refusal to supply or resupply arms (embargoes), can tip the scales in favor of one side, and, depending upon the circumstances, lead to negotiated settlement rather than escalated warfare—especially as the weaker side realizes that further fighting would be futile.

With a German colleague I have studied these effects for a series of wars in the Third World since 1960, mapping monthly patterns of arms acquisition during warfare. The results are summarized in Tables 3.1 and 3.2, the former for wars through the early 1980s and the latter for five conflicts of the early 1990s. The existence of arms embargoes and outcomes favoring one side or another, together with the pattern of negotiations for settlement of the wars, are noted and compared to the prewar arms advantages.

Our study found that embargoes generally had only weak impacts on the course and outcome of hostilities. In the Persian/Arabian Gulf (Iraq-Kuwait) and Falklands/Malvinas (United Kingdom–Argentina) wars as well as in some of the India-Pakistan fighting, for example, one side's weapon advantages ended the conflict well before embargoes took full effect. Warring states generally are able to offset supply disadvantages at least for a while by finding new, although often inferior, weapons sources. Embargoes therefore tend to favor the better-armed side.

Arms resupply affected the level of hostilities and the combatants' ability to resist negotiations in, for example, the former Yugoslavia, Sri Lanka, Ethiopia, and the Sudan. Over time, however, the diplomatic impact of arms transfers seems to have weakened with the rise of alternate arms suppliers on the international scene.[20]

These case studies lend support to the general conclusion that it is best not to deliver any weapons during a conflict unless a supplier favors one side to win if fighting should break out. Halting or denying deliveries may not prevent or stop the fighting, but more weapons clearly tend to

TABLE 3.1   The Impact of Arms Resupply on Outcomes of War, 1965–1982 Cases

War/Resupply[a]	Embargo[b]	Outcome[c]	Prewar Advantage[d]	Negotiations During War
1965 India-Pakistan				
Symmetric[e]	Symmetric: U.S., U.K.	Stalemate: India	Pakistan (qualitative)	Growing major power pressure to restrain parties
1969 El Salvador–Honduras				
None	Symmetric: U.S.	Stalemate: El Salvador	El Salvador (qualitative)	High pressure (OAS), delayed effect
1971 India-Pakistan				
Symmetric	Asymmetric: U.S. against Pakistan	India (mil.)	India (qualitative)	Major power pressure to restrain parties
1973 Arab states–Israel				
Symmetric	Threat: U.S., USSR	Advantage: Israel	None	Pressed by major powers, delayed effect
1976–1991 Morocco-Polisario				
Asymmetric: Morocco	Asymmetric: (only partial) U.S., France against Morocco	Morocco (mil.) Polisario (pol.)	Morocco	Major and regional power pressure, delayed effect, U.N. mediation
1977–1978 Ethiopia-Somalia				
Asymmetric: Ethiopia	Asymmetric: (informal) USSR against Somalia	Ethiopia	Somalia	Failed (OAU/Cuba/USSR), military intervention (Cuba)
1978–1979 Tanzania-Uganda				
Asymmetric:[f] Tanzania	Asymmetric: (informal) USSR against Uganda	Tanzania	Uganda	Failed (OAU), military intervention (Libya)
1980–1988 Iraq-Iran				
Asymmetric: Iraq	Asymmetric: U.S., EC against Iran	Stalemate	Iraq (just before war)	Failed attempts (Gulf states, U.N.), delayed effect
1982 Argentina-U.K.				
Asymmetric: U.K.	Asymmetric: EC, U.S. against Argentina	U.K.	U.K. (qualitative) Argentina (geographical)	Failed attempts (U.S., Peru, U.N.)

(*continues*)

TABLE 3.1 (*continued*)

War/ Resupply[a]	Embargo[b]	Outcome[c]	Prewar Advantage[d]	Negotiations During War
1982 Israel–Syria and PLO in Lebanon				
Symmetric	Asymmetric: (only partial) U.S. against Israel	Israel (mil.) Syria (pol.)	Israel	Multilateral/bilateral pressures, delayed effects, Western intervention

[a]In the column *resupply*, "symmetric" indicates that no combatant was favored; "asymmetric" indicates that the named party received substantially more arms.

[b]In the column *embargo*, arms embargoes were either threatened or actually put into effect (sometimes only partially, informally, or with insignificant results) by the suppliers named, either against all warring parties ("symmetric") or against the party mentioned ("asymmetric").

[c]In the column *outcome*, the wars ended with the victory of the named combatant or with a "stalemate" in which the named party had an advantage in military and/or political terms.

[d]In the column *prewar advantage*, the named combatants had an advantage before the war in the ability to fight, either with respect to all indicators or with respect to the quality or the quantity of arms.

[e]However, the U.S. tried to keep the Pakistani capability comparable to the Indian capability.

[f]Late in the war, Uganda received substantial arms supplies from Libya.

SOURCE: Frederic S. Pearson, Michael Brzoska, and Christer Crantz, "The Effects of Arms Transfers on Wars and Peace Negotiations," in *SIPRI Yearbook 1992: World Armaments and Disarmament* (Oxford: Oxford University Press, 1992), pp. 400–401.

make conflicts longer and bloodier. Sometimes defenders can be strengthened through arms supplies so that at least stalemate is achieved in the fighting and negotiations take place, but this generally takes a long time to achieve unless foreign soldiers are sent to intervene along with the arms. Arms transferred to achieve such defense also often end up being sold off to other wars.

Thus, in some circumstances one side can be strengthened to the point that it is able to survive; arguments for supplying arms to Bosnia in its tragic struggle with Serbian and Croatian nationalist forces in 1992–1994 were based on such reasoning. However, since there are many negative consequences from even such "successful" arms infusions (e.g., more civilian destruction and future revenge potential), it generally makes sense to seek international diplomatic pressure or, as a last resort, coordinated arms supply, multilateral comprehensive embargoes (including spare parts and all forms of civil and military trade), and military enforcement efforts, as through the U.N. Security Council, rather than sending arms unilaterally.[21]

Finally, the acquisition of arms to promote domestic security often leads to similarly disappointing outcomes. One need only remember the

TABLE 3.2 The Impact of Arms Resupply on Outcomes of War, 1991 Cases

War/ Resupply	Embargo	Outcome	Prewar Advantage	Negotiations During War
Iraq–Kuwait and coalition				
Asymmetric: Coalition (via weapon deployment)	Asymmetric: U.N. against Iraq	Coalition	Iraq (summer 1990) Coalition (from autumn 1990)	Failed U.N., French, Soviet efforts
Yugoslavia				
Asymmetric: Serbia (domestic arms production)	Symmetric: EC, U.S., U.N.	Stalemate: Serbia	Serbia	EC, Soviet, U.N. mediation with little success, U.N. peacekeeping agreed
Sri Lanka				
Asymmetric: Government	None	Stalemate: Government	Government	Failed direct negotiations, aborted Indian intervention
Myanmar				
Asymmetric: Government	None	Stalemate: Government	None	–
Sudan				
Symmetric	Asymmetric: U.S. (informal) against Government	Stalemate	Government	Failed OAU attempts

SOURCE: Frederic S. Pearson, Michael Brzoska, and Christer Crantz, "The Effects of Arms Transfers on Wars and Peace Negotiations," in *SIPRI Yearbook 1992: World Armaments and Disarmament* (Oxford: Oxford University Press, 1992), p. 413.

examples of the shah's Iran and the Soviet Union, two of the most heavily armed security states of their day, both of which crumbled from within as a result of domestic repression, excessive militarization, and resultant political corruption and opposition. Both states also were hurt by policy decisions that led to poor economic performance exacerbated by the waste of resources on military and industrial establishments, while large segments of the civilian public languished in comparative poverty.[22]

CONCLUSION

Since weapons buildups of various sorts do generally accompany wars, and since the question of the best path to peace is still open, global arms proliferation is a pressing concern for policymakers. We have seen that proliferation has proceeded, though not in a completely uncontrolled and escalating manner, and that arms represent fairly unreliable levers of diplomatic influence. Reportedly as many as twenty countries are now capable of producing nuclear weapons, but only six (the United States, the United Kingdom, Russia, France, China, and India) are known, through formal nuclear tests, to have done so, while three more (Israel, South Africa, and Pakistan) are now generally acknowledged to have followed suit even though they have not openly tested a weaponlike nuclear device. In 1992 South Africa claimed to have dismantled its weapons for fear of a new majority-rule government. There are political as well as economic costs in developing such threatening weapons, and not every state wishes to pay the price or take the risks.

Similarly, chemical and biological (toxic) weapons can be relatively easily developed but also entail risks. Some states, including the two superpowers, have reconsidered the worth of such potentially uncontrollable substances, especially if they should fall into terrorist hands. Other, smaller powers, however, see them as cost-justified in light of threats they perceive in their neighbors' and major powers' weapons, including nuclear weapons.

Although not every country has access to the latest arms, in the hands of determined fighters even primitive small arms can be exceedingly deadly. In the Honduras–El Salvador football war, heavy casualties for two such small countries were inflicted in hand-to-hand combat, sometimes involving machetes, while the two primitive air forces were soon grounded by lack of parts for their laughably old World War II–vintage planes.[23] The newest, most efficient weapons do not always kill the largest numbers, partly because they can be controlled more discriminately. Nevertheless, potent new weapons can open the way for massive destruction at the push of a button, for more efficient killing, especially since it is politically difficult to limit fighting and prolong the state of war. If **overkill** capabilities (i.e., excess destructive capabilities beyond what is reasonably and minimally necessary for protection) are available, leaders are tempted to use them to cover all contingencies and knock opponents out.

Evidently certain types of states facing certain political opponents or regional conditions tend to opt for specific types of arms. African states, with low arms budgets, few good roads, and broad expanses to patrol, have acquired many armored cars and transport vehicles. Middle Eastern states have imported vast quantities of tanks and jet fighters for the numerous dogfights and desert set-piece battles witnessed over the years. Open deserts leave massed troops more vulnerable to air attacks than do tropical rainforests (jungles) or rugged mountains. Advanced offensive equipment requires defensive countermeasures as well, so the latest anti-tank and surface-to-air missiles have been highly prized.

Given the largely negative record and policy pitfalls of attempted influence through either arms shipments or embargoes, the next chapter focuses on the history and relative success or failure of organized efforts to stem global arms developments and proliferation. On the one hand, as international institutions and laws have evolved, possibilities for cooperative agreements to limit the worst effects of arms trafficking have emerged. On the other hand, since anything relating to armament strikes at the very essence of national sovereignty, truly binding restrictions are extremely difficult to reach.

FOUR

□ □ □

Controlling the Spread of Arms

At the outset of the Reagan administration in the early 1980s, an influential U.S. policy adviser maintained that the only successful arms control agreement in history was the U.S.-British Rush-Bagot demilitarization of the Great Lakes in 1817.[1] Whether exaggerated or not, this skeptical perspective on arms control was to give way later in that administration to renewed cooperative U.S.-Soviet efforts to halt the nuclear arms race. That process finally culminated in the Bush administration with Strategic Arms Reduction treaties (START I and II), reducing by about two-thirds the number of nuclear warheads allowed to the United States and Russia (as successor to the USSR).

Although START did not fully contain the nuclear or mass destructive weapons race, when combined with agreements to prohibit development and deployment of biological and chemical weapons, to curtail drastically both conventional and nuclear forces in Europe, and to work toward limiting spread of conventional arms in certain other regions, the prospect for controlling arms proliferation appeared brighter in the early post–cold war era than ever before. Yet it remains far from certain that all the relevant actors and arms developments will be brought effectively into an international arms control regime.

President Ronald Reagan's early stance on arms was largely conditioned by his political reactions to the experiences of his predecessors during the Carter administration. President Jimmy Carter had attempted, at least on paper, some of history's most sweeping restrictions on the spread of arms, particularly on conventional arms. Citing the alarming U.S. tendency to arm dictators such as the shah of Iran, Carter placed annual ceilings (approximately $9 billion) on the value of U.S. arms exports through government channels and concurred with strengthened congressional regulations for notification and review of pending major arms deals. Thus, in legislation that raised constitutional controversy, Congress would have a veto opportunity.[2] Indeed, each proposed arms transfer was to be accompanied by an "arms control impact statement," complete with

71

reasons for the sale and its likely implications for U.S. interests and peace. Furthermore, Carter opened the Conventional Arms Transfer (CAT) talks, negotiations with the Soviets on limiting arms exports, concentrating initially on proposals for Latin America and Asia.[3]

Disillusionment soon set in, however, when it became clear that far from becoming "an exceptional foreign policy instrument," as Carter originally hoped, arms transfers were still considered integral to cementing cordial relations with key foreign governments. This was true especially when the United States was negotiating base and alliance or security agreements, as with the Philippines (under the authoritarian President Ferdinand Marcos), Spain, Turkey, Israel, Egypt, Pakistan, South Korea, Morocco, and Greece. Thus, certain countries and commercial sales were excluded from the arms ceilings, and new and somewhat deceptive accounting methods were employed to calculate the yearly totals.[4] CAT talks with the Soviets also got nowhere at that time because of competing cold war interests: Washington wanted Soviet arms out of Latin America; Moscow wanted the same for U.S. shipments to China; and neither could agree to resist the temptation to export to the Middle East and Africa.

As we have seen in previous chapters, the United States is not the only country to attempt unilateral, or even bilateral, restraints on arms transfers. Whenever restrictions are enunciated as working policy, however, ambiguities and loopholes abound. Even if interested in stemming the uncontrolled tide of foreign arms races, governments—especially those of major powers seeking both foreign influence and commercial returns—do not want to tie their own hands too tightly.

Carter's policy had two rather contradictory and vague objectives: (1) to facilitate transfers that "clearly promote" U.S. or allied security and (2) to restrain those transfers in excess of legitimate defense needs or those that "promote regional arms races or increase instability or otherwise do not advance U.S. interest."[5] How does one define "U.S. or allied security," "legitimate defense needs," or transfers that "increase instability"? Although one might presume that the best weapons should be reserved for the most trustworthy allies, such as NATO, even for the Carter administration the situation did not always work out that way, and decision-makers preferred to operate on a case-by-case basis.

Similarly, most arms-supplying states adopt case-by-case determinations. In the 1980s Britain wrestled with policies to avoid repetition of the Falklands/Malvinas dilemma, in which U.K. forces fought Argentina, a former client armed partly with British weapons; restrictions were aimed at denying arms to particular countries. Sales were barred on strategic grounds, for instance, to the Warsaw Pact (while it existed) and states with close ties to the pact or the IRA and to states embargoed by the United Nations for human rights concerns (i.e., South Africa, though arms and spare parts continued to trickle through via third parties or via classification for dual civilian-military use). Sales also were barred when they could hamper British diplomacy or military security (e.g., sales to Taiwan while relations with China were being developed; to Belize, the former British Guiana, during a dispute over its independence; and to Argentina).[6]

Seeking greater policy flexibility, German regulations also have been modified over the years to get around constitutional and policy restrictions regarding arms shipments to areas of tension—areas such as the Middle East that suffer or might suffer from warfare. Germany is a unique case in arms supply because of the stigma of its past aggressiveness under the Nazis. Legal language speaks of restraint on "lethal" weapons (as opposed to associated weapons systems). Over the years, areas-of-tension constraints have been modified to allow exceptions based on political considerations or the "vital interest of the Federal Republic [FRG]" so long as "existing tensions" are not heightened or supplies sent to "countries where there is the danger of an outbreak of armed conflict."[7] Even with such provisions, however, German arms found their way to hot spots such as the Iran-Iraq War during the 1980s.

Thus, most major powers express some concern about heightening the chances of war abroad but hedge their arms regulations with provisions to allow sales and transfers to favored clients or in profitable circumstances. U.S., U.K., and German rules have spoken vaguely, for example, of resisting the introduction of new or destabilizing weapons technologies to certain regions. All three claim to favor sales within NATO over those involving less secure regions. But all three have also continued to ship advanced arms to "reliable" friends in such volatile areas as the Persian Gulf and South Asia and have sometimes ignored human rights violations and other annoyances in doing so. Again the twin goals of security and welfare—in varying proportions for different suppliers—make arms shipments a policy option difficult to resist.

In this chapter the history of efforts to control the arms traffic and bring some order or predictability to the competitive process of supplying weapons is explored. I look at history as a key to what might work in this difficult policy domain in the future, noting the pitfalls and success stories of past efforts and comparing them to the emerging multilateral arms control agenda and to unilateral or bilateral moves to limit the availability of arms.

THE EMERGENCE OF ARMS CONTROL

One of the earliest recorded efforts to achieve political and security accords related to armament were the fifth-century B.C. negotiations between the Greek rivals Athens and Sparta wherein the latter asked the former not to build improved fortifications around its city. Although technically this would not have limited what we know as weapons, it would have controlled the size of Athenian city walls, which would have reassured Sparta about the stability of their mutual competition and showed that Athens did not intend to gain a telling strategic advantage; thus theoretically peace would have been promoted. Similar psychology and reasoning rationalized the mutual nuclear deterrence doctrines pursued by the United States in recent years, known as **mutual assured destruction,** in which both sides sought to maintain stable capabilities to assure the total destruction of each other's population. In both cases assurance was sought that the opponent would leave its population as a sort of hostage, vulnerable to attack, in order to assure mutual good behavior and nonaggression. However, as skeptics of arms control might have expected, Athens deceived Sparta in their negotiations, hurrying to complete the ramparts and using the talks only to stall. Ultimately Sparta saw no alternative but war, and its forces took twenty-seven more years to breach the Athenian fortifications.[8]

Ironically, just as demand for new arms can grow during and after wars, historically arms restrictions and even disarmament have been most feasible and prevalent after wars, crises, or conquest. Sometimes the winner simply enforces a period of disarmament on the loser and maintains it for as long as possible. Such was the case, for example, in the Treaty of Zama, Rome's 201 B.C. effort to limit Carthage's total of ships and elephants as well as to destroy its city walls. Similarly, Napoleon forced army size limits on Prussia in the 1806 Treaty of Tilsit, and wide-ranging disarmament was stipulated for the losers in both World Wars I and II.[9] Clearly, such one-sided restrictions usually last only as long as the power disparity lasts; once states recover from war or find new allies, they generally try to rearm, at least to an extent, and then it is up to their opponents to stop them, which seldom proves feasible. As with Tokyo and Washington in recent years, former enemies can become allies, and the formerly disarmed state might be encouraged by its ally to take on more military responsibility than it might otherwise even want.[10]

Apart from enforced unilateral disarmament, the only other viable route appears to be bi- or multilateral agreement. There are no evident historical cases of voluntary complete unilateral disarmament. A twelfth-century German prince did renounce the use of the crossbow, but he reversed the decision after thirteen years when it finally became evident that none of his adversaries would reciprocate the gesture. Similarly, because the Soviet Union did not reciprocate the unilateral U.S. elimination of chemical weapons production in 1969, it appears that in 1985 Washington pushed for renewed production to add pressure for a negotiated treaty.[11] However, Mikhail Gorbachev's unilateral Soviet initiatives in the late 1980s to

BOX 4.1 Bilateral and Multilateral Arms Agreements

Among bilateral agreements, in addition to those dealing with the U.S.-Canadian border, one could note historically the Anglo-French Naval Pact in the eighteenth century (1787), Ottoman-Egyptian arms limitation in the nineteenth (1841), and U.S.-Soviet SALT nuclear accords in the twentieth (1969–1975). A number of early arms control agreements set limits on weapon deployments: the Peace of Callais in 448 B.C., which restricted the movement of Athenian and Persian war vessels in the Aegean Sea; the Treaty of Kuchuk Kainarji between Russia and Turkey in 1774, which prohibited Turkish fortification of the Crimean Peninsula near Russian territory; demilitarization, or removal of forces, along the Swedish-Norwegian border in the Karlstad Convention of 1905; and demilitarization in the Turkish Straits under the Lausanne Convention of 1923 (subsequently renegotiated and maintained between the Soviet Union and Turkey).

The Brussels Act of 1890 (for repression of the slave trade) was the first multilateral agreement specifically to address the international arms trade; its effective implementation was dubious, however. Among the most famous subsequent multilateral arrangements were the Hague conferences on disarmament and the laws of war, in 1899 and 1907, where dumdum (expanding) bullets and some lethal gases were banned (leaving many other potent weapons intact). These were followed by the 1925 convention banning the use, though not the development, of gas warfare.

SOURCES: Christopher J. Lamb, *How to Think About Arms Control, Disarmament, and Defense* (Englewood Cliffs, NJ: Prentice-Hall, 1988), p. 44; David G. Anderson, "The International Arms Trade: Regulating Conventional Arms Transfers in the Aftermath of the Gulf War," *American University Journal of International Law and Policy* 7 (Summer 1992): 759.

observe a complete (above and below ground) nuclear test moratorium, though far from disarmament, did help build an atmosphere of trust and public pressure on the Reagan-Bush administrations that probably facilitated agreements on arms reduction. Some strategic theorists have suggested such limited unilateral initiatives as a way to reverse the momentum of arms buildups; one such theory was labeled GRIT, graduated and reciprocated initiative in tension-reduction.[12]

Negotiated arms control and disarmament treaties have been far more frequent than unilateral cuts. Some of the forms of such agreements are outlined in Box 4.1. As seen in these examples, arms control can take many forms. Demilitarized zones and multilateral restraint on weapons emplacements have been attached to many wartime cease-fires or peace treaties, as in the contemporary Middle East between Israel and its neighbors (agreements frequently broken) and the neutralization of Austria after World War II. Some arms control pacts limited the number of weapons allowed—for example, the 1924 Convention on the Limitation of Armaments of Central American States set restrictions on army sizes and numbers of warplanes and ships in the area. Others were meant to control the type, deployment, or characteristics of weapons—for example, the 1890 Brussels Act restrained updated firearms and ammunition in Africa to reduce slave trading.[13]

With the age of multilateral **intergovernmental organizations (IGOs)**— world or regional organizations, such as the League of Nations after World War I, with nation-states as members seeking jointly to address or solve outstanding diplomatic, economic, or social problems—disarmament goals and periodic meetings were written into the IGOs' charters and agendas. Especially between the world wars, many citizens advocated disarmament as an avenue to peace; avoiding outright weapons bans, the great powers responded with the Washington and London Naval treaties of the 1920s and 1930s as well as the Kellogg-Briand Peace Pact, the latter of which outlawed war as a policy instrument but nevertheless contained numerous reservations and loopholes. The naval treaties set ratios of various nations' acceptable fleets of battleships and cruisers, requiring parties to dismantle some war vessels. The experience left ambitious rising powers such as Germany and Japan highly frustrated at being given smaller arms quotas than established but perhaps declining powers such as Britain. Skeptics have noted that the motivations for such exercises may have been more monetary than military—attempting to limit costs in a constant arms race, while leaving unresolved the basic rivalries that during the 1930s would doom the agreements.[14]

The League of Nations also established machinery to follow up the earlier Brussels Act on slavery and legally regulate the international arms traffic. The St. Germain Convention was designed to control arms transfers to Africa, Turkey, and the Middle East, though most of its provisions were never implemented, partly because of the absence of the United States from the League.[15] Another ambitious sounding control scheme was the 1925 Convention for the Supervision of the International Trade in Arms and Ammunition and in Implements of War (the Geneva Arms Traffic Convention, for short), which sought to please Washington by leaving regulation to the individual participating states rather than the League of Nations and emphasizing mainly publicity of arms deals rather than arms production. Too few states signed the agreement, however, and it too never entered into force.[16]

Nevertheless, as part of these efforts, the League did manage to institute a registry of the weapons trade designed to list and thus expose major arms deals and encourage restraint. Fifteen annual registries were published. Both the League and United Nations went further still, voting arms embargoes of certain states as a form of sanctions against international aggression (e.g., embargoes against Italy and Japan in the 1930s) or domestic repression (e.g., South Africa from the 1960s to the 1990s).[17] Even though these measures aided those trying to keep track of weapons shipments and in some cases raised the cost of violent behavior, they were largely symbolic in nature and did not prevent continued arms shipments, violations of the law, or World War II.

The registry approach recently has been revived with the establishment of an annual U.N. arms register to detail arms trading, shipments, and receipts. Some strong advocates of such reports, like Britain, argue that arms transfer **transparency** (i.e., the opening of arms deals to public scrutiny, data collection, and reports) embarrasses arms suppliers that fail to comply and counteracts terrorism by proclaiming where arms are supposed to be going officially so that diversions can be detected. Although a surprising number of countries (more than seventy as of 1993) have turned over information on arms shipments to the new registry, many arms recipients still oppose transparency because it would open their arsenals to scrutiny and accounting or because it would supposedly compromise the dealings of their arms manufacturers. Armament statistics thus remain basically in the hands of individual governments.[18]

Another approach to arms control negotiations has been by regional or geographic focus. In certain areas, generally those not of prime strategic concern to major powers, suppliers and in some cases recipients can agree to keep armament levels limited to avoid undue advantage for any party. Among such locations have been Antarctica, demilitarized by treaty in 1959; Latin America and the Caribbean, declared a **nuclear-free zone** by treaty in 1967; the South Pacific, where eight states, including Australia and New Zealand, followed suit in 1985; outer space, off limits to orbital weapons of mass destruction by treaty since 1967; and the deep seabed, where, according to a 1971 treaty, no weapons of mass destruction can be installed.[19]

Latin American states also pioneered in regional efforts to control the importation of conventional arms. In the 1974 Declaration of Ayacucho, eight Andean countries sought to agree on stabilizing and cost-saving limits to imported arms and military technology. As yet, however, these limits represent only aspirations rather than a binding treaty.[20]

Even though the hope for regional or universal disarmament has been expressed at various times by world organizations, peace advocates, pacifists, religious leaders, and utopians, until recently it seemed that the prospects of beating swords into plowshares were quite remote, especially in the relations of big powers. Rather, it seemed more prudent and practical to settle for limits and restrictions on the number, size, development, or deployment of weapons, what has come to be called arms control. Hence the Strategic Arms Limitation Talks (SALT) of the late 1960s and early 1970s and the NPT of the same era were aimed basically at preventing further growth or the spread of certain weapons, generally those considered relatively obsolete or destabilizing, rather than eliminating existing stockpiles.

Elimination of some systems came rather unexpectedly, however, with the **Intermediate Nuclear Forces** and CFE agreements and START in the late 1980s and early 1990s. Here, finally with mutual inspection, the United States and the Soviet Union/Russia agreed to dismantle or remove particularly threatening weapon systems. The earlier antiballistic missile and later chemical/biological treaties also ban classes of weapons and open the way for debate about whether exotic ideas such as the **Strategic Defense Initiative** ("Star Wars" space-based antimissile weapons) or short-range Patriot-type antimissile systems are allowable. Nevertheless, much of the newer and threatening weapons technology has neither been restrained nor eliminated.

Arms agreements are effective only so long as they are in the participants' interests. For example, few, if any, states had contemplated installing weapons in Antarctica or on the seabed prior to the agreement on treaties concerning these areas; in contrast, the Latin American nuclear-free zone has been criticized because the states with the greatest nuclear potential, Argentina and Brazil, have not joined. Nevertheless, since major powers agreed to respect and not destabilize nuclear-free zones, such precedents have encouraged discussion of similar arrangements in places such as the Pacific, the Balkans, the Indian Ocean, Central Europe, and Scandinavia.

As arms and technologies have spread and more countries have become independent, increasing major power attention has been paid to nonproliferation agreements (restraints on the introduction or spread of feared weapons) such as the NPT of 1970. Major powers see uncontrolled proliferation as a threat to international predictability and "order." In some conventional arms agreements, suppliers have resolved not to allow certain types of arms shipments to certain recipients; often, as we saw in the last chapter, such supplier restraint comes just before, during, or after wars in the form of embargoes designed to dampen hostilities or keep them from getting out of control. Classic cases were the U.S.-British-French agreement not to supply arms to Israel and its Arab opponents in 1950 and the Anglo-U.S. arms cutoff to India and Pakistan during their 1965 crisis and war over the Kashmir region. Although somewhat effective, such embargoes, including those involving human rights abusers (e.g., Chile, Argentina, South Africa), generally favor one side more than another (India had readier access to alternate suppliers and was less exclusively dependent on the United States and United Kingdom than was Pakistan) and stimulate greater efforts to build or acquire weapons independently (India, Israel, Argentina, Chile, and South Africa all developed indigenous weapons production after embargoes or supplier restrictions).

Arms recipients sometimes see nonproliferation efforts as discriminatory—as favoring states that are already powerful. Nevertheless, antiproliferation moves commonly involve mutual agreement between suppliers and recipients. These might be agreements to limit **vertical proliferation** (the escalation of weapons technologies and sophistication) or the more common **horizontal proliferation** (the spread of weapons to more countries). In the nuclear area, for example, the most notable horizontal agreement was the NPT, a complex accord whereby the major powers pledged to restrict their own nuclear arsenals (hence the SALT accords) and make "peaceful" nuclear technology available to the Third World. Potential nuclear states vowed in return not to acquire the weapons and to allow **onsite inspection,** visits to known or suspected weapons laboratories or sites by IAEA officials to account for the use of weapons-grade fuels such as plutonium at the nuclear facilities of these states.

One flaw in such agreements, as with the regional agreements noted earlier, is the likelihood that those states most capable of and intent upon acquiring the weapons, such as Israel, Pakistan, Argentina, Brazil, or North Korea, will not sign or abide by them. Also, determining the limits of peaceful versus military technology can be difficult in nonproliferation accords, as the fuels or by-products from one process can be used in another. Over the years, NPT cheaters have been discovered, as in Iraq's advanced nuclear weapons program. Although North Korea issued an ominous threat to become the first state formally to withdraw from the NPT in 1993 in a dispute over inspection of its nuclear facilities, the treaty nevertheless was unprecedented in obtaining and retaining the consent of more than one hundred states not to acquire or supply a highly destructive form of armament.

What can or should the international community do to suspected cheaters? At this point it appears that concerted pressure, especially by major powers, is the most that can be hoped for. Israel resorted to "self-help" in the early 1980s by attacking an Iraqi nuclear research reactor with air strikes. This action delayed but did not end Baghdad's nuclear preparations. The later U.S. attacks on Iraq during the Gulf War in 1991 went a step further. But if France and those that had facilitated Iraqi nuclear research had insisted on more effective inspections earlier, some of these confrontations might have been averted. U.S. efforts to enlist China in a campaign to force open North Korea's nuclear facilities are just such a joint diplomatic approach combining sanctions with inducements. In the process, of course, states must keep their priorities straight. Washington, for example, would have to decide whether it valued Chinese cooperation on arms control more than Chinese compliance with domestic human rights standards (an issue over which the United States threatened to cut trade relations). Washington also would have to balance pressures on North Korea with effective security arrangements and agreements for the Korean peninsula and Japan to avoid provoking a renewed Korean war. Thus, arms negotiations can never be separated from the larger pattern of political and security policy and negotiations.[21]

CHALLENGES AND REQUIREMENTS FOR GENERAL ARMS CONTROL

From what we know about arms control and disarmament processes historically, they are based on three major motivations: fear, trust, and cooperation. Mutual fear of destruction, bred of long-term arms competition, can lead to pragmatic agreements to forego the use or development of certain weapons or to keep such weapons within reassuring limits and out of the hands of unreliable groups. In plain terms, the accumulation of arms sometimes becomes too explosive to tolerate.

In part, this is what happened in the early 1980s as newer, faster nuclear delivery systems were introduced into the crowded European continent, and as **multiple independently targeted reentry vehicles (MIRVs)** (warheads or multiple bombs atop missiles, with each bomb programmed to hit a separate target) mushroomed in superpower arsenals. President Reagan was widely quoted as saying that he could even conceive of a possible "limited" nuclear war in Europe. The nuclear disarmament movement, begun in the 1950s as the "ban the bomb" campaign (source of the famous trident peace symbol), was revived with efforts such as the **nuclear-freeze campaign,** which aimed to halt the addition of more weapons. Grassroots pressure, including city council resolutions, peace marches and sit-ins, and statements by religious leaders, brought concerted pressure on national governments to reach arms reduction agreements.

To work, such accords had to be based on a modicum of mutual trust, such that participants did not expect treachery or at least that one side's cheating could be detected and punished easily enough by the other. Here we get the concept of **verification,** in which methods of reassurance and inspection, even if not foolproof and even if conducted by remote sensors rather than on-site inspectors, are acceptable.[22] Recognition of mutual fear or need for arms limits, plus growing mutual trust, facilitates an atmosphere of cooperation and tempers conflict.

By affording parties to an arms agreement the technical means to check up on each other, verification machinery, ranging from spy satellites to

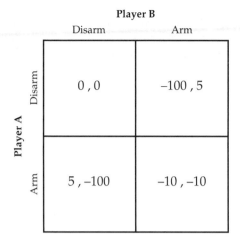

FIGURE 4.1 The Prisoner's Dilemma of Arms Races.
Payoffs to A are shown at left, and to B at right.

human spies, allows escape from the arms control stalemate of the so-called Prisoner's Dilemma game (Figure 4.1). Here the two adversaries (labeled A and B) would be better off (note the various hypothetical payoffs in the matrix) by mutually disarming, but they cannot trust each other sufficiently to take the first step for fear of the massive potential cost of a sneak attack. Therefore, they both generally end up worse off by continuing to arm, with mounting defense bills.

In his START negotiations with President Gorbachev, President Reagan quoted an old Russian proverb: "Trust but verify." In a sense, verification both depends on and allows trust, enabling states more willingly to risk even unilateral arms restraint.

Arms control and verification initiatives, then, have both symbolic/political and military security payoffs, just as we saw in Chapter 1 with the development of weapons themselves. Politically such provisions, even if subject to some cheating and incomplete coverage, at least tend to define standards to which states can be held accountable and contribute to an overall sense of trust and deescalating tensions and costs (or distrust and mounting tensions if violations are detected). More stringent verification and compliance may be required for stricter military security.

Technical verification alone may not be sufficient to assure the success of arms control initiatives if they are not seen to be in the parties' political interest. For example, seismographs, developed for earthquake research, also are able to detect nuclear test explosions at long distance. Yet despite this capability, during the 1950s the United States demanded on-site inspection of Soviet nuclear test facilities in any test ban agreement, a condition Washington knew the spy-sensitive Soviets would reject. A combination of factors finally broke the negotiation stalemate and allowed the above ground (atmospheric) nuclear test ban of 1963. These included conclusion of the main series of U.S. nuclear tests, development of the Nevada underground nuclear test site, and the mutual U.S.-Soviet fears brought on by the Cuban missile crisis confrontation of 1962.

The continued effectiveness of such agreements depends on all sides remaining satisfied with the political outcome and security guarantees of mutual compliance, confident of the inspection process and safeguards against unauthorized third parties stealing weapons or their components. Therefore, international control agencies such as the IAEA become necessary to oversee and verify compliance; even then, some uncertainties and controversies are likely to remain.[23] IAEA, for example, has been criticized for lax nuclear inspections, understaffing, and lenient rules for judging suspicious states such as Iraq and North Korea. Yet these agencies can be no more effective than is allowed by the governments that create, fund, and host them.

Two international agreements of the early 1990s, one bilateral and one multilateral, offer hope regarding the future of arms control and disarmament; both involve weapons of mass destruction rather than conventional weapons. The first is START II, concluded, pending ratification, in early 1993 to cut by an additional one-third the number of land-based nuclear warheads available to the United States and Russia (and other former Soviet republics). To cinch the agreement, certain concessions were made to satisfy both worried Russian nationalists and the U.S. Congress. Reducing the number of strategic warheads on each side to the three to four thousand range, this accord went far toward redressing the problems caused by MIRVs in the 1970s. Nevertheless, considerable nuclear weaponry remains, and the stability of Russia and other former Soviet republics, some of which were nuclear armed, remains in doubt. For example, Ukraine, despite stated intentions to dismantle its nuclear arsenal, has delayed while outstanding security problems such as border and ethnic disputes with Moscow remain unresolved and until the economic outlook improves. French, Chinese, and British nuclear arsenals, though themselves cut or restricted for budgetary reasons as well as modernized in recent years, also are not yet covered under the START process; nor are the weapons of regional powers such as Israel, India, Pakistan, or South Africa.

Even in peaceful nuclear electricity programs, such as Japan's, large amounts of plutonium and weapons-grade fuel are manufactured. No fully reliable global monitoring, accounting, and reporting system on the production, storage, and distribution of such fuels now exists. The task is beyond the current resources of the IAEA. It has been estimated that at five to seven kilograms of plutonium per bomb, the potential for thousands of basic nuclear weapons exists worldwide in such plutonium production as well as in the recycling of plutonium from existing or dismantled nuclear bombs.[24]

The second important new agreement is even more ambitious; the result of more than twenty years of negotiation, it involves complete chemical weapons disarmament. More than 110 countries agreed in early 1993 to ban the production, possession, and use of chemical arms, going much further than the use ban of 1925. As in START II, rigorous on-site inspection provisions were included, which in the case of chemical arms are complicated by the multitude of factories and laboratories engaging in chemical production. Awaiting ratification by a minimum of 65 countries, the Chemical Weapons Convention (CWC) is expected to become effective sometime after January 1995.

Penalties in the form of economic or military sanctions are to be imposed on states found violating the CWC agreement, and violations can be detected through both regular and on-demand verification inspections. In the latter case, challenge inspections cannot be refused. Yet such inspections will require establishing a massive international bureaucracy; said one chemical arms analyst, "The paperwork is going to be enough to choke a computer."[25]

Worried about losing power relative to Israel and its reputed nuclear weapons program, a number of Arab states have refused to sign CWC, and both China and Pakistan have expressed reservations. But those not signing face sanctions and quite severe restrictions on chemical supplies and technologies. Although facilities ranging from old weapons sites and military factories to chemical and insecticide plants must be monitored, CWC provisions have been labeled "about as foolproof as one gets in the disarmament field."[26] Unlike nuclear weapons, chemical arms have been used in recent years (e.g., Iraq against its Kurdish minority), and establishing a momentum for eliminating these devices, even if some of the major users and threats remain, is important for further negotiations on nuclear and conventional arms.

Now that considerable progress has been achieved in the areas of chemical and biological arms control and disarmament, intermediate and short-range nuclear and conventional weapons in Europe and Asia, and long-range strategic nuclear weapons (START I and II), the most conspicuous and controversial challenges remain in the areas of nuclear proliferation, weapons testing, space weapons, and conventional arms. Airborne and short-range U.S. and allied nuclear forces also remain in Europe without a definitive target, and effective enforcement of new agreements and progress in dismantling weapons must be watched closely in the period of rapid change among former Soviet republics. Russia has asked its Western treaty partners to permit its redeployment of arms and forces south toward ethnically diverse former Soviet republics. The Western allies have had some qualms about agreeing to these moves, which might equip Moscow to intervene in and manipulate the politics of these territories, though NATO powers also recognize the importance of stability on Russia's borders.

An atmospheric (above ground) nuclear weapon test ban has held since 1963, attracting additional adherents in France and China, but nuclear weapons are still tested underground. Two schools of thought contend over the future of these tests: one arguing that they are needed to improve the safety and security of weapons through introduction of new technologies and the other arguing that to eliminate the means to improve nuclear weapons would eventually lead to their demise. Largely because of pressures generated by President Gorbachev's unilateral test moratorium of the early 1980s, the superpowers resumed (stalled since 1974) negotiations on a threshold test ban treaty (TTBT), eliminating underground tests of more than 150 kiloton explosive yield (with both on-site and seismic verification procedures). Agreement on the TTBT was reached in 1990, another step toward a comprehensive nuclear test ban, but conflict with China and France over the issue soon stalled progress. Nevertheless, such a ban could be a key issue in the renewal talks for the NPT in 1995 since the majority of the world's nations will want to know that the major powers are continuing progress toward nuclear disarmament.[27]

One approach to promoting trust is through what are termed **confidence-building measures,** which are procedures to reassure worried enemies that military preparations and maneuvers are not indications of an impending attack. When invited to observe rivals' training exercises, or when offered opportunities to meet and discuss security concerns, states presumably become more willing to forego or lay down portions of their armaments. Alternative security guarantees also could be offered by major powers. Yet the capability of such powers, even of the United States, to reassure worried governments such as Ukraine or Pakistan remains quite limited. The West's inability to end the prolonged fighting in the former Yugoslavia is only one troubling precedent. Therefore, resort to "self-help" through armament, even nuclear armament, remains a live alternative for many governments.

One other factor—the search for new technology—limits arms control prospects; this is the same factor that drives the armament process. Going all the way back in history, states generally have been most willing to forego and restrict arms that were already outmoded or no longer needed, while racing ahead to develop the latest equipment or preserve prestige arms such as battleships (even after the latter had performed poorly in wartime) or trusted warhorses such as main battle tanks.[28] Thus, when

TABLE 4.1   Current, Multilateral Arms Control Regimes

Regime	Specific Agreements
Mass destructive weapons accords	Nuclear, biological, chemical (e.g., START, NPT, CWC)
Missile Technology Control Regime	Agreement (beginning in 1983) among various powers to consult and limit the export of ballistic missile technology, especially nuclear-capable delivery systems
Coordinating Committee on Multilateral Export Controls	Cold war–era agreement among Western powers to restrict flow of sensitive military technology to the East; now modified to seek restrictions on high-tech transfers to threatening LDCs
Conventional arms transfer controls (evolving)	Consultation mainly among the Big Five permanent members of the U.N. Security Council

SOURCE: Leonard S. Spector and Virginia Foran, *Preventing Weapons Proliferation: Should Regimes Be Combined?* Report of 32nd Strategy for Peace, U.S. Foreign Policy Conference (Warrenton, VA: Stanley Foundation, October 1992), p. 5; supplemented by material from Martin Navias, "Ballistic Missile Proliferation in the Third World," *Adelphi Papers* 252 (Summer 1990).

SALT I set numerical limits on U.S. and USSR long-range nuclear delivery vehicles (missiles and bombers), the race continued for several more years to see which side could pile more warheads on those launchers or guide the warheads more accurately to targets.

PROSPECTS FOR LIMITS ON THE SPREAD OF WEAPONS

To summarize what we have seen about arms limitations, the world currently relies on four primary multilateral regimes concerned with limiting the spread of threatening military capabilities; the four are outlined in Table 4.1. The first, dealing with three sorts of mass destructive weapons, involves nonproliferation or disarmament agreements, seeking unconditional limits on the production and availability of these horrifying devices. The other three categories of agreements involve not freezes or elimination of the spread of weapons, but attempts to slow or restrain it within certain limits; these have been called regulated trade regimes.[29]

The stronger form (binding treaties) of the mass destructive weapon regime is due primarily to the greater psychological fear and loathing these weapons produce. Their use threatens to upset international force balances and is gradually becoming less tolerable to influential segments of the international community, or at least to the major powers. Missiles, new arms technologies (e.g., dual use computers), and conventional weapons, however, generally do not yet elicit that level of revulsion and therefore are traded and transferred with fewer intrusive controls. Attempted controls on the missile trade are growing, but one wonders why missiles seem more terrible or threatening than bomber aircraft—which also are able to deliver mass destructive bombs and which can be traded relatively freely. Perhaps it is that bombers are more expensive than missiles, thereby naturally limiting their availability; missiles can be small, portable, relatively cheap, accurate without risking human pilots and crews, and therefore a more prevalent threat in world politics.

The emerging question for arms control, then, is whether the four main regimes can or should be combined to form a more binding and coherent U.N. arms inspection, regulation, and restriction system. Indeed, in 1991 the five major powers—the United States, United Kingdom, France, Russia, and China—agreed to the principle of restraint and mutual consultation in releasing destabilizing weapons (particularly guided missiles) to volatile regions such as the Middle East. Yet just a few months later, media headlines were trumpeting the continued sale of Chinese and Korean missiles and Russian submarines to Iran, along with record U.S. arms agreements with Saudi Arabia, Kuwait, and Israel.

Hopes for a more orderly world were jarred by the reality of rising ethnic tensions and the disintegration of more states, such as Yugoslavia and Czechoslovakia, with severe pressures on others such as Liberia, Angola, Burundi, Zaire, the Congo, Sudan, Somalia, Afghanistan, Iraq, India, and Sri Lanka. More factions within states have become armed, as, for example, in the emergence of a peasant rebel group in southern Mexico in 1994. Some governments continue to crack down hard on their ethnic minorities, as in Indonesia's military campaigns in East Timor.

The United Nations and other regional international organizations (e.g., the OAS and the Organization of African Unity [OAU]) are hard pressed to take on increasingly difficult responsibilities for humanitarian relief, peacekeeping (keeping warring sides apart), or peacemaking (promoting peace settlements) in the midst of such disputes and chaos. These agencies still lack well-trained standing military forces of their own and can only reflect the consensus their members are able to achieve on any given crisis. Scenes of Somalia, Bosnia, or the former Soviet Georgia as armed camps, where looting, banditry, pogroms, and protection rackets become major enterprises, recall the horrors of Beirut during the 1980s as well as the World War II Holocaust and three-year German sieges of Russian cities. Would-be peacekeepers are reminded of the difficulty of disarming warring factions to promote stability and peace.

As peace came to some troubled lands, such as Nicaragua and Namibia in the late 1980s, relatively successful factional disarmament took place under U.N. or international supervision; militia units traded at least some of their weapons, usually the oldest and most tattered, for jeans, T-shirts, and cooking oil. Yet they also reportedly sold their more desirable arms and hoarded or buried the rest for possible future use.[30] Arms control and peacekeeping both require constant vigilance, occasional neutral third-party mediation, and tireless negotiations to relieve underlying tensions, provide reassurance, and keep track of devious weapons traffic.

On the encouraging side is the fact that major arms transfers have remained relatively concentrated among relatively few countries; almost half of the Third World major arms flow in the 1980s was directed at just five: Iraq, Egypt, India, Saudi Arabia, and Syria.[31] Beyond that, for nearly a decade the total international arms trade market has been declining, at least by best estimates. Some arms-producing companies, thinking twice about shrinking defense budgets and slumping markets, have abandoned or deemphasized the business. In general, weapons manufacturers are consolidating, specializing, and merging, even across national lines. It has been estimated that 75–80 percent of existing U.S. weapons contractors, including small subcontractors, could be "swallowed up by more aggressive industry leaders or simply leave the market by the end of the [1990s]."[32]

Even though arms sales totals have dipped, renewed supplier efforts and interests, driven by the relentless pressure to export, show considerable potential for another rise—though a rise confined by long-term global economic recession. This again complicates the ability to track and limit arms transfers. In the future, the possible addition of as many as 100 or more new ethnically based nation-states to the 180 already in existence, the reality of cash-starved arms-producing countries and firms competing to export weapons and generate new markets, and the availability of cheaply produced higher-technology arms (e.g., portable missiles) could be the primary challenges to arms control.

Though most potential arms recipients cannot afford major armament, they also remain suspicious of major power arrangements to limit arms supplies, tending to see them as a paternalistic threat to sovereignty designed to maintain the weapons technology gap that disadvantages the less developed countries. The emergence of major powers again willing to aid regional recipients for strategic purposes could also restart arms races despite a lingering economic and credit crunch.

Arms control agreements presuppose the existence of stable governments in control of the weapons trade and able to enter into binding treaties or agreements. The reality of shaky regimes and ethnic discontent, along with multinational arms production among manufacturers, undermines these expectations.[33] Agreements to limit the arms trade furthermore must satisfy governments' and especially suppliers' underlying strategic and economic goals: "to sustain domestic military production and employment, improve trade balances, retain at least some autono-

"IT WAS MADE AT THE OLD TRIDENT MISSILE PLANT!"

The pitfalls of converted arms production. By permission of Wayne Stayskal for the *Tampa Tribune*. Reprinted in *Washington Post Weekly* (National edition) (August 1993).

mous arms manufacturing capabilities, and curry favour with influential Third World regimes."[34]

As we learned in previous chapters, one key to the spread of arms is their rate of production since excess production generally must be sold off through exports. The end of the cold war and sagging international arms markets brought renewed hope that swords could indeed be beaten into plowshares, that defense production, running in high gear since World War II, could finally give way or be converted to consumer production. Competing interests of government, manufacturers, workers, peace advocates, and world organizations are involved in the debate over **defense conversion.** Occasionally these interests converge in agreements to cut back on arms while at least preserving enough defense manufacturing capability to meet armed forces' needs at cost-efficient prices. As seen in Box 4.2, such agreements and successful conversion projects still remain elusive, however.

Despite the difficulties of implementation, it is at least possible to list the types of agreements and arrangements that appear necessary to control weapon proliferation:

1. To assure a viable level of purchases from various defense manufacturers while fostering multinational and multifirm manufacturing cooperation to eliminate overcapacity and excess production in defense manufacturing,[35] presumably without stifling weapon quality and price competition or creating undue arms dependence on single suppliers

2. To show that the major powers are reducing arms inventories so as not to constitute an imperialistic threat to weaker states, while at the same time providing sufficient forces for deterrence, defense of victims of attack, enforcement of international law, humanitarian or pacification purposes, and multilateral peacekeeping[36]

3. To keep overall arms levels and technology in regions within certain agreed (between suppliers and regional powers) ratios—remembering as well that sometimes greater supplies of less sophisticated arms (e.g., machine guns, artillery, and helicopters) can kill more people than fewer copies of the most advanced and expensive equipment (e.g., latest jet fighters)[37]

Clearly, certain types of weapons still must be produced in relatively large amounts, while other systems can be reduced or eliminated. International peacekeeping, for example, will require fast and reliable troop and equipment transports, both for air- and sealift, as well as armored vehicles and electronic battlefield control. Nuclear attack forces, revamped battleships, and hunter-killer submarines, together with supersophisticated radar-evading craft, might be too expensive and impractical for most situations.

It therefore becomes feasible, but still politically tricky, to think of a more "managed" supply of arms tailored for and dispatched to those in acute need of defense and withheld from "overarmed" clients or war zones. Some strategists also have suggested linking development assistance to disarmament or taxing arms transfers to generate development funds (though risks of smuggling grow with such measures), thus rewarding states that reduce defense expenditures the most or maintain them at low levels. This proposal runs into opposition, however, both from arms purchasers and supplying states interested in fostering their arms industries.[38]

The precedent of major power arms transfer consultation also could be furthered, especially among security partners such as NATO states. The latter traditionally have been reluctant to extend collaboration outside of Western Europe, but out-of-area concerns are growing and are increasingly shared by the United States, Britain, France, and Germany as they undertake joint military and peacekeeping operations in locations such as the Persian Gulf and Africa.[39] As noted, consultation among the broader

BOX 4.2 The Defense Industry Conversion Debate

Pro

As U.S. defense spending slows, countless businesses struggle to convert from military contracting to peacetime pursuits. The switch can be particularly taxing for small enterprises, which often lack financial resources to go very far afield. [Defense contractor] Micro Kinetics's move into two diverse areas—display advertising and engine-cleaning machines—suggests that a successful transition from swords to plowshares takes money, the right niche, a savvy investor—and a bit of luck. ...

The firm's financial crisis worsened during 1991. ... Early last year, [venture capitalist Adrian Gluck] introduced Micro Kinetics to an electronic advertising display being developed by Admotion Corp., ... [a] firm in which Mr. Gluck had invested $3.1 million.

Admotion's displays needed more precise engineering. (Designed for malls, the plastic gizmo resembles a television set but works like a moveable billboard. ...)

By last October ... a second prototype worked well enough to attract orders from Kraft General Foods Inc.; ... PepsiCo Inc.'s Taco Bell unit; and several other firms. ...

The company isn't relying solely on the display-sign venture. Last year, Micro Kinetics paid an undisclosed amount for the car engine-cleaning unit of Carbon-Clean International, a Norton, Ohio company. ... The maker of machines that remove carbon pollutants from engines was renamed MotorVac Technologies Inc. Micro Kinetics now sells over 250 MotorVac machines a month—for up to $3000 each.

Micro Kinetics also is developing robotics devices and, in the wake of the World Trade Center bombing, a consumer smoke mask based on a military model.

Though it's too early to predict Micro Kinetics's long-term success, company officials see early signs of a payoff. Employment is rising again.

Con

Defense conversion seems to promise a way to avoid layoffs, plant closings and business failures. There are roughly 9,000 primary suppliers of defense products in more than 200 industry segments. Together, they constitute approximately 3 percent of the [U.S.] gross national product. Further, the technology base of these companies is very sophisticated. Helping them convert their resources to new endeavors, *and* helping the economy, seems like a win-win proposition. Unfortunately, the facts say otherwise.

First, the coming defense cuts, and their effect on procurement and research and development, dwarf the size of conversion markets. ... The markets for typical conversion products—like wind-shear detectors [for airports] and night-vision equipment—are minuscule compared with the Pentagon's former defense needs. ...

Second, defense-oriented companies have an abysmal record of conversion. ... There were simple reasons why ... capable companies did not succeed. Either they did not know the business or market they were entering, or their advantage in skill, technology or product was not sufficient to bring about success. ...

□ When defense contractors have successfully diversified, rarely has the source of competitive advantage rested on technology ... from the military side of the business.

□ Joint ventures, licensing or outright sale have provided the highest return to the shareholders in those few cases when a government-contracted technology or product has been brought to the commercial market successfully. ...

□ Successful conversion of physical capacity—especially fixtures and tooling—is extremely difficult.

□ Conversion, when successful, has taken decades.

□ The more unfamiliar the product or market, the higher the likelihood of failure. ...

The real task for the companies in the defense industry is to get on with the difficult and painful process of restructuring— ... selling businesses to "natural owners" ... merging companies in areas of declining demand ... concentrating in certain business segments in order to become a premier competitor. ...

In the end, the task is not converting the defense industry from military to commercial markets but changing the industry: from one made up of diversified defense contractors in too many declining segments to one made up of highly focused companies in sustainable segments.

SOURCES: Sarah Lubman, "Small Defense Firm Unearths Plowshares," *Wall Street Journal*, March 17, 1993; Jerrold T. Lundquist, "The False Promise of Defense Conversion," *Wall Street Journal*, March 18, 1993. Reprinted by permission of *Wall Street Journal*, © 1993 Dow Jones & Company, Inc. All rights reserved worldwide.

group of permanent U.N. Security Council members—the Big Five—has been tried since 1991 but has proven troublesome. Group members agreed to keep one another informed of major arms deals and to consult on limits, particularly regarding Middle Eastern armament. However, the agreement was strained immediately by a U.S. jet fighter sale to Taiwan, which led to China's threat to withdraw from the regime. Even China does not want to be seen as a rogue elephant on the issue of arms proliferation, however, especially as Beijing seeks to reassure neighbors about its peaceful intentions, about the future of Hong Kong, and about the prospect of good trade relations.

Therefore, a number of further remedies have been proposed, including:

1. The resumption and expansion of CAT talks to include all major arms-supplying and recipient states, perhaps initially seeking mutual ceilings on shipments or restraint in certain regions or on certain technologies;
2. An enhanced MTCR, which would expand the consultation on export of ballistic missile technology begun in 1987 among the United Kingdom, Canada, France, Italy, Japan, Germany, and the United States to include the likes of China, Brazil, and Russia and thereby ban transfer of missiles capable of delivering nuclear weapons and provide for verification;
3. The establishment of regular consultation and negotiations among traditional rivals (India-Pakistan, Israel-Syria, North and South Korea, Greece-Turkey, etc.) and their major power arms suppliers, seeking agreed regional arms control and security pacts; and
4. The linking of development aid and technology transfers to arms and military spending limits, that is, to so-called **conditionality** provisions.[40]

CONCLUSION

By now we can cite pitfalls in each of the arms control approaches. For example, multilateral arrangements such as MTCR still are often nonbinding and without the force of law or treaty.[41] There is no foolproof way to prevent arms trafficking, smuggling, or noncompliance with agreements. Yet arms control and disarmament momentum can build when economic costs mount, when fears of arms races rise, when trust develops, when security can be assured, and when cooperation pays off.

Certain principles for an arms transfer control regime are clear even if the details are yet to be worked out: (1) rationalize arms production through multinational consortia of manufacturers to reduce excess production while sustaining competition; (2) show progress on reducing major power armament and arsenals; (3) strengthen multilateral security and peacekeeping guarantees and capabilities; (4) maintain regional arms and related technology levels within agreed limits through joint supplier-client consultation; (5) provide managed and appropriate arms supplies to those in dire need of defense (with provisions against reexports to other warring parties), while withholding supplies from overarmed or reckless states (difficulties of definition noted); (6) experiment with new incentives such as increased development assistance in return for arms reduction or an arms trade tax to finance development; (7) establish more intrusive, though politically negotiated, verification of arms levels and greater transparency through improved reporting and uniform categories of arms and arms component transfers.

Among the models commonly proposed or tried to achieve these goals are (1) unilateral restraint by individual governments, which generally amounts to case-by-case reviews of specific arms sales; (2) multilateral supplier cartels to establish arms transfer guidelines, an approach that benefits those already armed; (3) piecemeal restraint on certain weapons or regions (such as CFE or MTCR talks); (4) recipient initiatives, such as the Declaration of Ayacucho; (5) substitution of aid for arms imports; (6) transparency initiatives involving voluntary or compulsory reporting of arms transfers; and (7) treaties, perhaps on the model of the NPT, that would combine some of these approaches and provide for legal enforcement and penalties.[42]

Traditionally in the arms control field, one side was most favorable to limiting advances in weapons technologies in which it already held a lead or for which it had little further use. Greatest opposition existed to agreements that would cut weapons of most potential use or perceived strategic importance. Since arms control is a political process, with leaders responsible to their constituents whether in the public or the military, this continues to be the case in many respects.

But the pattern also is changing with the shift in Russian and U.S. priorities to civilian-based economic and technological advancement and with global economic problems. Greater willingness to slash excess defense spending and production is evident across the globe; some companies are finding the weapons business insufficiently rewarding or stable, while others lop off nondefense enterprises to focus more intensely on military production. Of course, even those shifting investments to such promising civilian sectors as telecommunications and computing could be keeping a hand in both military and commercial fields through dual use technology. It is still easiest to justify government spending for "national security."

If U.N. crisis control and peacekeeping machinery are to be effective, warring political groups' easy access to weapons must end. Meanwhile, however, the continued lure of new arms technology breakthroughs and many states' perceived needs to intervene abroad in the interest of regional resources, influence, and global order preserve many aspects of the arms race mentality. In the next chapter, the strange simultaneous pattern of arms restraint and spread is further explored in an effort to resolve the major dilemmas of international armament.

FIVE

□ □ □

Conclusion: Can the Dilemmas Be Resolved?

B oth change and continuity are present in the post–cold war global arms spread. Change is evident in factors such as:

□ The reform and breakup of the USSR and the lessening of superpower tensions, which have led to new agreements on regional issues and to some limitation or reduction of weapons of mass destruction;

□ New U.N. assertiveness on issues formerly considered to be domestic or too controversial for the world organization, including provisions such as a new arms transfer registry and on-site weapons inspections;

□ Economic difficulties and full arsenals, which have resulted in diminished world arms markets and budgets;

□ Trade of weapon components and technology instead of weapons per se; and

□ The strong psychological and battlefield impact of high-technology arms, whose costs evidently reduce their use potential in some cases.

Continuity is reflected in some of these very changes as well as in other factors:

□ The former USSR and Eastern bloc as well as Western states and LDCs such as India, China, and North Korea remain under heavy economic pressure to sell weapons abroad.

□ New arms control agreements revive controversies over such issues as on-site inspection and unfair advantages or double standards for one side or another in access to arms.

□ Nuclear arms arsenals in Europe, North America, and Asia remain troubling.

□ New U.N. responsibilities revive familiar qualms about giving strategic and military decisionmaking power to the world organization as well as about having to fight for peace.

□ The dip in world arms spending could be reversed with emerging regional and ethnic conflicts and the search for cheaper suppliers of higher-technology weapons.

□ Weapons technology, including nuclear technology, continues to trickle down from more to less advanced states, and both black and gray arms markets thrive.[1]

In other words, then, even though progress has been made toward limiting the development and deployment of some weapons, toward reducing overkill capacities, agreements still leave large gaps wherein major powers can develop modernized arms, including nuclear or space-based systems, and regional powers can still try to obtain them. Technology continues to march on, threatening further to destabilize political relations. It may soon be possible, for example, to launch precise conventional weapons attacks on opponents, with self-guiding missiles flying through a specific window in a presidential palace.[2] What does this portend for political trust or confidence building or for deterrence (i.e., the ability of one side to frighten its opponents enough to dissuade them from attacking)?

Perhaps such developments are inevitable. There is as yet no foolproof path to disarmament or to shutting off the development and distribution of new arms technologies. Nevertheless, in this concluding chapter we can look for signs of progress toward resolution of the various armament dilemmas described in the Introduction.

For example, on the positive side of the emerging weapons picture is the continuation of confidence-building measures in agreements such as the CFE Treaty. Even in the midst of uncertainties about which European states adhere to the treaty's arms limits, it promises to relieve tension by opening troop and force deployments for inspection and maintaining frequent communications concerning threats. With the treaty and possible reduction of surplus arms, however, Europe as a whole, with all its unresolved ethnic and nationalist conflict, continues to "hold the largest conglomeration of advanced conventional arms in the world,"[3] and many of these spill over into the arms trade.

One related challenge for the future of arms control will be monitoring and facilitating the promised dismantling of former Soviet and U.S. nuclear weapons under the START agreements reviewed in Chapter 4. The sheer difficulty of reclaiming the tons of uranium and plutonium from nuclear arsenals as they are scaled back defies both arms control and defense

Disassembly of U.S. nuclear warheads in Amarillo, Texas, 1993. (Photograph Jim Wilson/NYT Pictures, October 31, 1993, p. 1.)

cost containment. "Dismantling nuclear warheads may be infinitely better than detonating them, but the job is tricky. In addition to being radioactive, plutonium is highly toxic and can burn on contact with air, and most of the explosives [used as detonators] are old and prone to detonate with heat or shock."[4]

Washington has promised financial and technical aid to the hard-pressed Russian Republic in disposing of weapons and in finding other tasks for arms scientists and technicians so they are not tempted to peddle

BOX 5.1 Mounting Indian-Pakistani Weapons and Tension

Recent weapons transfers, and announcements of arms purchases, have aggravated long-standing tension between India and Pakistan. These weapons systems, combined with persistent strife over Kashmir and increased nuclear weapons capacity, have caused relations to degenerate to what some say is their worst state in decades. ...

The rancor between India and Pakistan has its origin in religious disputes. ... The Kashmir conflict [on their border] is the continuation of that animosity [as both sides claim the predominantly Muslim territory]. ...

With advanced weapons and an armed force twice the size of Pakistan's, India has what one observer termed "a colossus," compared to Pakistan's forces ... [and] despite ailing economies, the two countries continue to spend large sums on defense.

Indeed, while India's economic growth dropped about 40% from 1989 to 1991 and its debt rose over 20% in the same period, defense spending kept pace with inflation and will be approximately 13% of the total budget in 1994. Pakistan, one of the world's poorer countries, will spend about $3.3 billion on defense in 1994, which is an estimated 35% of its budget.

... Both countries have embarked on what appears to be a tit-for-tat deployment of de-stabilizing offensive weapons. ... Pakistan is said to have taken delivery of M-11 surface-to-surface missile technology from China; ... India said two of its own missiles would be operational [in 1993]. The Prithvi, a short-range, surface-to-surface missile, was reportedly deployed on the Pakistan border. ...

Also, after Russia succumbed to U.S. pressure and canceled a $350 million contract with India to supply cryogenic rocket engines, India vowed to develop its own. ...

their services widely around the world. But the aid at times has been slow to arrive (because of bureaucratic inertia among three U.S. agencies concerned, and because of budgetary and political uncertainties about the general subject of aid to the former USSR); and Congress has attempted to add restrictions making further Russian assistance conditional on negotiations to stop Moscow's arms sales to such countries as Iran.[5] The Russians themselves have been at pains to come to terms with suspicious neighboring republics, now countries, which formerly housed Soviet strategic nuclear forces.

Projections for the future also show other regional arms races heating up, particularly, as seen in Box 5.1, in Asia. In the Indian-Pakistani competition, one can see all the arms transfer and control trends and dilemmas highlighted in this volume.

Both nations have said they may deploy additional tanks. ... Pakistan began discussions with England to buy 300 used Chieftain battle tanks ... and ... India's Arjun tank successfully completed a round of firing exercises. ... India announced it was also putting Russia's $2 million T-80U tank through trials. ...

Acquisitions by India [in 1993] include 1,200 artillery pieces, 100,000 AK-47 rifles and 15,000 anti-tank mines. India is also negotiating with Israel for an upgrade package on 100 MiG-21 fighters, and the Indian cabinet has approved a $1 billion purchase of 80 combat-ready trainer aircraft. Pakistan's buys are more modest but include six British frigates armed with surface-to-surface and surface-to-air missiles.

The very act of buying and deploying new weapons has become a de-stabilizing factor in the region. ... [Pakistani experts argue that] India's justification for its force levels "is that they have to face China, but most of the troops are along the Pakistani border."... India's sea power is also disturbing "because of the possibility of a naval blockade."...

Badly outnumbered in conventional forces, Pakistan has turned to the nuclear option for protection. This move ... has not helped Pakistan's defensive capability. [According to experts,] nuclear weapons development has made Pakistan "less secure because, should a war start due to India's insecurity, it would be total."...

Some confidence-building measures have been implemented over the past few years in an attempt to decrease tensions, however. In 1988, each country agreed not to attack the other's nuclear facilities. And, since 1990, six rounds of talks on military issues have produced two agreements. Each country agreed to respect the other's air space and to provide advance notification of military exercises.

SOURCE: "Kashmir, Weapons Fuel Indian-Pakistani Tensions," *Arms Trade News* (August-September 1993): 1–2.

A GLIMPSE AT THE FUTURE OF WEAPONRY

As we move toward the next century, there are already clear indications of the type and quantity of weapons to be expected. The legacy of the Gulf War and the era of tight budgets are driving these developments. In addition, the switch from arms to consumer production has been neither very easy nor complete given the time, effort, and investment needed to retool and retrain workers, uncertain markets, and the temptation of continued profits through arms.

As the world's leader in military technology, the United States continues investing in the next generation of supersophisticated computer, stealth, and electronically controlled weapons, which will, if they work as expected, increase firepower while reducing vulnerability and the need for human operators. Evidently there is also a tendency to exploit new

The "technology demonstration vehicle" Sea Shadow, built by Lockheed Missiles and Space Company in the mid-1980s, began its first daylight testing off the coast of southern California in 1993. The vehicle was developed to explore a variety of advanced technologies that can be applied to surface ships. (Photograph courtesy of Lockheed Missiles and Space Company, Inc.)

technologies from one type of weapon in other types, as when advanced stealth aircraft designs are copied in naval vessels. Besides each military service's desire for the "latest and best" technology, the effort now is to fulfill the triple goals of reducing a state's own while raising the "enemy's" prospective battle casualties, cutting armed force personnel costs, and keeping advanced military industries in business, though possibly at reduced employment or "higher productivity" levels.

In the U.S. arsenal, new smart weapons are expected to include tanks and artillery as well as naval (e.g., automated destroyers requiring smaller crews) and aerospace systems. "The Army's future tank is expected to be a 50 ton vehicle built mainly of composite materials with a two-man crew and a 120mm gun. Advanced vehicle command, control and communication systems that provide instantaneous intelligence and data distribution will yield weapons that are easier to operate and more effective."[6]

Skeptics might argue that we have heard these stories before and that such costly superweapons could be ill-suited to the varied new missions that armies are likely to encounter in the next century—such as sensitive peacekeeping or humanitarian relief, as seen in the former Yugoslavia or Somalia. High-technology armor may or may not be needed in such circumstances, as compared to quick transport capabilities and improved observation and scanning equipment. One might also doubt that stealth concepts from aircraft can be translated easily to other arenas, such as the realities of sea battles. In the past, concerns surfaced about the long-term reliability or breakdown rate of highly sophisticated equipment such as automated tank gun loaders as well as their vulnerability to relatively simple countermeasures such as guided missiles.

The feats of countermeasures also can be exaggerated, however; there still is no agreement, for example, on whether the U.S. Patriot antimissile system succeeded in knocking down the bulk of incoming Iraqi Scud missiles attacking Israel and Saudi Arabia. Yet it does appear, from both the Gulf War and Falklands/Malvinas experience, that if one side possesses a clear and overwhelming advantage in advanced systems, such as space-based battlefield surveillance, electronic communications and weapon control, and airpower, it will prevail rather easily over its opponent militarily, if not politically (Hussein remained in power in Baghdad despite his crushing military defeat in 1991). The United States' agreement in 1993 to share its main military communication satellites with NATO allies points up the priority of plugging modern weapons into a common "eye in the sky" for the new "electronic battlefield."

Cost and the potential lure of civilian high technology are further factors in plans for the next generation of arms. Recall that each U.S. B-2 Stealth bomber costs in excess of $700 million, so that the loss of even one plane becomes a very costly consideration. Depending on the price of the new equipment, therefore, the U.S. government might be hard pressed to order sufficient quantities to make production efficient. At the same time, the sophisticated technology might be too sensitive to export abroad to enlarge the market, even to NATO allies if Europe becomes more independent or produces its own new tanks or planes to compete with U.S. models. In considering tanks, for example, the alliance might have to agree on joint production or purchase of a single "multinational" model and then in relatively small numbers since the vast Soviet tank arsenal is no longer poised across the Iron Curtain.[7]

One "solution" to these dilemmas of cost and capability becomes tempting: designing and testing the next generation of heavy weapons in the laboratory, utilizing computer simulations and a few prototypes, but building and ordering very few copies until they are needed in crisis. Cheaper and simpler self-guided missiles or aircraft and older, more expendable equipment might be substituted for the latest expensive systems at the front. Whole generations of advanced arms could therefore spend their "useful life" on the shelf, never being mass produced and never seeing battle unless other equipment failed.[8] More money would be thrown into military research and development, with less thrown into production. The feasibility of this approach for military readiness and ease of conversion to defense production in crisis is untested, and it could rob the civilian economy of needed investment funds.

Cost-cutting considerations have several additional potential military effects. One might be to lower the threshold of nuclear war in some circumstances, as in disputes among smaller states. If it becomes too costly to maintain armed forces in high readiness, or if smaller cash-strapped countries such as Ukraine or Pakistan confront a big neighbor such as Russia or India over border or ethnic disputes, reliance on cheaper and deadly nuclear weapons could grow for deterrence or, ultimately, defense.[9] Russia's reaction to China's growing military and economic power along their long common border also remains uncertain and potentially disruptive.

One further troubling consideration is the potential psychological effects of the new weapon systems. If we recall that arms are sometimes meant to deter opponents rather than be used for attack, their future deterrent value could be reduced by higher technology. They might be too valuable to use, which could promote a form of restraint in warfare; therefore, certain ambitious opponents could be tempted to risk a confrontation thinking their enemy would withhold its best equipment. Furthermore, if fewer soldiers are required for military missions while more firepower is generated through mechanized weapons, there might be less political restraint on leaders wishing to launch wars. They would no longer be so pressed to justify the conflict as worth the lives of the troops. Again, the consequences could go either way: Potential enemies or challengers could become more worried, thus bolstering deterrence of their attacks, but the country with the more mechanized forces itself could become more emboldened and aggressive.

These science fiction–like, alarming scenarios are further complicated by the future lure of civilian technology. For example, the United States is now said to lead the world in high-resolution television (featuring much higher-quality TV pictures), a field previously expected to have been dominated by Japan. There is much talk of sophisticated telecommunications "superhighways," combining computers, telephones, and TV to process pictures and information simultaneously either for business or the household. This seems to be a civilian technology wave of the future.

Yet historically such breakthroughs, including space technology, electronics, computing, and nuclear power, saw discoveries used at least as heavily for military as for civilian purposes; indeed the discoveries often took place in military labs, with later civilian applications. Depending upon the extent and direction of government funding and contract demands, it is therefore likely that corporations seeking the most extensive markets and profits will produce equipment with flexible potential both for combat and consumers. They might seek to design components meant to be usable in military or civilian systems almost interchangeably, thus complicating arms control challenges.[10]

DILEMMAS AND THE CHANGING INTERNATIONAL SYSTEM

Many uncertainties therefore remain about the future value and effect of weapons systems in a world approaching two hundred independent nation-states. We have seen one question renewed in the Bosnian aspect of the Yugoslav wars of the 1990s, for example: the dilemma of whether to provide more arms to the side that appears to be the victim of aggression.[11] In theory, such aid should make it possible to rebalance a conflict and discourage the parties about their chances of military success, thus hastening a negotiated solution. This view is an offshoot of the old theory of peace through a balance of forces or power. Such balances require a level of precision in arms supply, however—just enough to discourage and not enough to escalate the fighting—which can prove most elusive in practice.

As the debate on Bosnia unfolded at the United Nations and in national capitals, the great complexities and dilemmas of arms distribution came once again to light. The besieged Muslims were not entirely at a loss for weapons since they had inherited many from the Yugoslav (mostly Serbian) army when it left for Belgrade; therefore the old question of how much is enough resurfaced. Also, it was argued that more arms for the Bosnians would just reheat the war, sending it to new levels of escalation as the Serbs too would step up the illicit arms trade despite the continuing arms embargo. One reported worry was that the Russians were all too ready to open the weapons supply spigot to their Serbian friends.[12] Therefore, the uncertainties of the security dilemma (Prisoner's Dilemma in Chapter 4) also resurfaced.

The question of whether to ship arms depends in large part on the goals being sought. A psychological impact on enemies or friends can be achieved in a relatively short time merely by agreeing to such shipments, though this impact can vary, including possibilities of generating countershipments from other sources. Military impacts, as we saw in

Chapter 3, can be slower; in some wars arms supplies have taken up to five years to have effect, as troops finally learn to employ them effectively. Supplies also seem most effective when followed by formal military intervention by the supplier to bolster its clients' forces and teach them how to employ the equipment most effectively. Yet formal outside military intervention deepens and complicates a crisis or war.

And, finally, it appears that one cannot have peacekeeping and arms balancing at the same time. Indeed, one of the prime duties of peacekeepers, as seen in Somalia, is often to disarm the combatants since arms infusions can generate more fighting and complicate the peacekeeper's job of separating parties, arranging truces, and protecting refugees and civilians. In Bosnia, one of the prime worries about sending in more arms and following up with NATO air strikes (intervention) was that U.N. and NATO peacekeeping forces might come under heavy retaliatory fire from the non-Muslim side.

Nevertheless, the memory persists that strategically timed arms shipments helped swing the tide of battle against the Nazis in World War II (U.S. Lend-Lease shipments to Britain and Russia, which were risky given German U-boat attacks but judged worth the cost) and against the Russian invaders of Afghanistan and Somali invaders of Ethiopia in the 1980s. Therefore, "peace through armament" is still a tempting policy choice.

One has to look carefully at the circumstances of individual conflicts in order to decide whether arms shipments make sense. Political dynamics and outcomes must be examined in order to solve the armaments dilemmas. For example, Afghani rebels were able to shoot down Soviet helicopters thanks to an infusion of U.S. Stinger anti-aircraft missiles in their long civil war. U.S. arms did the trick in helping defeat the Soviet interveners, though not necessarily in promoting a stable regime in Kabul. Arms shipments also seemed to offset any pressure (weak as it would have been) for U.S. forces to intervene and confront the Soviets directly.

Yet one also has to ask at what cost in policy terms. Afghanistan continued undergoing civil war and disruption among the rebel forces themselves even after the Russians left. The Soviet Union collapsed after the war, an outcome still debated in terms of its potential for global disruption. The Stinger missiles reportedly fell into the hands of the Iranians, evidently through their connections to the staunchly Muslim Afghan rebels, just as U.S. naval forces arrived in the Gulf to protect shipping during the Iran-Iraq War. When U.S. forces confronted the Iranians, there was thus the risk of facing those same missiles, another example of the access dilemma. In toting up whether the anti-Soviet policy in Afghanistan was "worth it," even at the relatively cheap price of some Stingers, reasonable people can still disagree.

The political dilemma of armament concerns the difficulty of political influence through arms transfers or the use of force and the necessity of political control over weapon transfers. Again regarding Afghanistan, it has been observed that

> Afghanistan, ... the last proxy war of the East-West confrontation, revealed how the superpowers' sway has diminished. First, Muslim guerrillas equipped with American weapons humiliated the mighty Soviet army and forced it to withdraw; then they turned on their American benefactors and rejected Washington's advice on a political settlement. Now Afghanistan, one of the poorest countries on Earth, is under the control of neither superpower. "We can't deliver our Afghans," a harried U.S. diplomat said, "and they can't deliver theirs." ... "The ability of outsiders to influence events is generally declining," said Richard Haass, a former Harvard professor now on the National Security Council staff. "There are simply too many sources of wealth, technology and arms for either the United States or the Soviet Union to be in a position to dictate local decisions. ... Denial of military or local support is thus a less credible sanction than it was. So is the threat to intervene."[13]

Arms given to affect either foreign outcomes or behavior frequently fail to do so. One of the key reasons may be the structure of the international system at any given time.[14] Currently the world is changing or transforming from a bipolar superpower structure to a more diverse and open structure, with U.S. military power predominating but several independent military and economic powers exercising significant regional clout. The implications of these changes for the dilemmas of armament are still being worked out:

□ Access to arms appears likely to increase for many states and armed groups, at least in the short run, with more arms sources and fewer political limits on who is an acceptable client. Yet most arms-dealing governments increasingly demand cash payment instead of credit sales.

□ The dilemma of alternatives to arms production as a ticket to higher technology and profits remains unresolved; manufacturer consolidations, mergers, and co-production agreements appear far more likely in the coming years, which should gradually reduce excess production and the urgency to export.

□ Weapons appear ever more lethal as technology spreads, complicating the war causation dilemma by increasing both potential deterrence and recklessness.

□ The dilemma of adequacy promises to play itself out, along with the security dilemma, in regional arms races as long as arms budgets hold out and until international negotiations, peace treaties and agreements, or organizations set reasonable limits and promote security.

☐ Political dilemmas become primary, especially in the necessity to find peaceful solutions to ethnic and boundary disputes; major and minor powers alike must stand ready to enforce those regional agreements and arms limits.

Another short-run consequence of the cold war's end is the growing freelance nature of the arms business.[15] Central governmental control of weapon transfers appears more difficult or more lax in a number of states. For example, in the search for foreign exchange, a small cadre of Chinese army officials and a few party bureaucrats evidently have been authorized to promote arms sales on their own initiative and use the proceeds to fund military modernization projects. Even though governments may increasingly appreciate the political sensitivity and risk of the arms trade, their ability to restrain it might be eroding for both economic and political reasons.

Nevertheless, the advent of costly high technology may be setting natural limits to arms transfers, even as political limits may be more problematic. Well-armed states such as Taiwan and Israel have settled for lesser but still advanced equipment in the 1990s (e.g., F-16 instead of F-18 U.S. fighters), partly for fear of stimulating an ever-greater high-tech regional arms race, and partly for reasons of cost.[16]

We have seen that the nature of the global arms trade remains both capital intensive and dependency generating. Although developing countries now import the technology to produce arms (starting with licenses) as well as the arms themselves,[17] the trade in components and spares still perpetuates a good deal of dependence on suppliers. This increasingly is a two-way street of interdependence as suppliers also need the foreign markets and as arms also afford the recipient the possibility of triggering wars that cause difficulties and concerns for the arms suppliers (as in the former Yugoslavia). Recipients also now insist on various forms of compensation from sellers for the high cost of weapon purchases; these compensations are usually referred to as **offsets** and **countertrade,** with the former including agreements to transfer valuable technology to the buyer and the latter involving agreements to purchase products from the buyer. The classic example of countertrade was the "great ham giveaway" by McDonnell Douglas at Christmastime a few years ago: Danish hams, which the company was obliged to purchase in return for aircraft sales to Denmark, were given as gifts to employees.

Thus, arms transfers complicate political and economic relations by affording recipients somewhat greater freedom of action while perpetuating interdependence and supplier involvement.[18] This interdependence reinforces the conclusion that international arms transfer controls must be premised on agreements both among suppliers and between them and arms recipients.

This book's historical review has shown that the arms trade is built into development of both industrial technology and political competition. Keith Krause has argued that the world since the 1970s is in fact reverting to some of the older competitive patterns, as contrasted to the peculiarly frozen nature of the U.S.-Soviet cold war years (for example, the reemergence of old and deadly rivalries in Central and Eastern Europe).[19] States are once again freer to search for arms from competing and consolidated commercial sources but also have less assurance of finding arms through superpower political competition. The political utility or benefit of arms transfers appears to be in decline,[20] while governments retain interest in regulating what manufacturers sell abroad. Fewer payoffs in political co-operation, U.N. voting, or reliable influence over events or recipients appears possible if arms recipients are no longer forced to choose between East and West.

This raises hopes that at least one motive for weapons transfers—the security policy motive—finally may be weakening. Even as governments set records for arms sales for a combination of commercial gain and regional power balancing, they may be seeing more clearly now the political and military pitfalls involved. Indeed, if recent efforts by the United States and Russia to convert their defense economies pay off, the other motive for arms sales, economic benefits, could also weaken.

It is unlikely that arms transfers will disappear, however, as long as weapons are produced in a sovereign state system; yet preferences for other types of technology could displace and reduce them in the long run. In the short run, efforts to set rules of the road for transfer, such as those proposed at a policymaker conference on the arms trade (see Box 5.2), appear to be ever more crucial. "The trends emerging in this current system toward commercialization, the internationalization of defense production, illegal arms trade, and trade in dual-use and upgrade packages will continue to put pressure on ... governments to control the negative consequences of the arms trade."[21]

Note, however, that the policy community is far from sold on the best remedies and approaches. For example, some advisers and members of Congress counseled President Clinton to reverse the Bush administration ban on weapons (F-16) sales to Indonesia in 1993. That ban, which included refusing permission for U.S. fighter jet sales from Jordan, had been aimed at the Suharto government's extensive reputation for human rights violations in the former Portuguese colony of East Timor. U.S. officials worried, however, that to withhold arms for such reasons was "1960s

"And the Lord said, 'They shall gradually, so as not to cause unemployment, beat their swords into plowshares.'"

The slow way out of the weapons business. Drawing by Dana Fradon; © 1993 The New Yorker Magazine, Inc.

thinking''—tactics that would have little effect in an era of multiple arms suppliers. In addition to shopping elsewhere, an irritated Indonesia, one of the largest countries in the world, supposedly would be less likely to cooperate with U.S. policy in Asia, especially regarding China. It was speculated that Indonesia itself might break up, à la Yugoslavia, if it were denied needed arms to crush rebellions. Yet these arguments were countered by others in Congress who pointed out that the furtherance of human rights demanded as much of a stance against Indonesia as it had against South Africa and that countries requiring military repression to stay together might not be good bets anyway.[22]

CONCLUSION

Who should be armed and to what extent? Certainly independent members of the international system of nations retain the sole legitimate political right to arm; U.N. machinery could inherit a similar right if its charter provisions on a standing army were activated. Similarly, in the future organizations such as the EC, Arab Gulf Cooperation Council, or Association of Southeast Asian Nations could firmly unify their security policy. No legal armament right exists for dissident groups, aggressors, or terrorists, but many suppliers who believe in the justice of these groups' causes or the color of their money continue to provision them. Aside from the nuclear, chemical, and bacteriological weapons categories, arms limits are not yet set by law or even by political agreement; yet they are evolving through fear, the reality of arms inefficiency, and costs.

For the first time in history, it appears that the multilateral arms control and selective disarmament doors are open. When the five Security Council powers met to negotiate principles of restraint in 1991, it was the first such gathering since the brief bilateral CAT talks of 1978 and the tripower restrictions toward the Middle East in 1950. The latter agreement was breached by the upstart USSR (jointly with Czechoslovakia) in a 1955 arms deal for Egypt. Although Russia, China, North Korea, Israel, or others could still play the upstart role today, arms restraint is possible given the continued agreement of the Security Council powers. Such agreements, of course, have their share of critics and skeptics, as noted in Box 5.3.

Although nothing even approaching a formal arms restraint regime resulted from the 1991 talks, the symbolism of the statement of joint principles, voluntary rules, and consultation was the key to future coordination.[23] Limited machinery, such as the consultative missile and technology control groups, is in place to provide a forum for efforts to limit the spread of arms. The success of these endeavors will determine whether new control mechanisms are developed for more types of conventional weapons.

When they competitively armed their respective clients and allies during the cold war, Washington and Moscow still maintained their own tacit understandings and restrictions (e.g., not allowing Middle Eastern clients to wipe each other out). Now the five powers are groping toward new understandings and limits, if not an outright reduction of the arms trade itself. Such a reduction, already under way for financial reasons, can be expanded only with solutions to major regional conflicts, the cooperation and agreement of smaller regional powers, and the strengthening of international organizations and verification processes (as in the CWC model for chemical weapons).

Arms are a commodity more available to the wealthy than to the poor states of the world, but their impact affects everyone. Likewise, sound policy regarding the dilemmas of armament requires the participation of the full array of actors and interest groups involved in the "weapons game"; it must entail more than merely symbolic gestures toward arms

---

BOX 5.2 Conference Recommendations:
The Arms Trade in a Transitional Economy

The following recommendations stem from an unofficial U.S.-CIS (Commonwealth of Independent States) Security Dialogue held in Washington, DC, in May 1993. Conference participants included legislators and staff, executive officials, representatives from the ministries of defense and foreign affairs, and members of the nongovernmental expert community from the United States, Russia, Ukraine, and Kazakhstan. The report was signed by a group of U.S. researchers at the conference; they endorsed the general thrust of the recommendations but were not necessarily unanimous on each point.

1. The United States and other supplier countries should recognize that widespread sales of advanced conventional weaponry—while presenting short-term economic benefits—present long-term threats to international peace, stability, and security. ... [They] should conduct a full *security* cost-benefit analysis of any proposed arms export, in addition to an economic cost-benefit analysis. The effect of arms exports on stated military and foreign policy goals should be carefully considered.

2. Arms industries in the supplier countries should be discouraged by their governments from looking towards exports as an alternative to defense conversion. Toward that end, the United States should enter into discussions with other major arms exporting nations about eliminating government subsidies for arms exports and possibly putting the monies saved into a conversion fund that could be made available to countries that are making a good faith effort to reduce their arms exports.

3. One of the few transparency measures for monitoring the arms trade now in place is the United Nations Register on Conventional Arms. To improve the effectiveness of the Register, the major supplier countries should condition their arms sales on recipients' participation in the Register. ...

4. Both supplier and recipient countries should work through the United Nations and other multi-lateral political institutions to design regional mechanisms to reduce military forces as an alternative to regional arms build-ups. ...

5. The United States should immediately lead an effort to re-start discussions among the leading exporters on limiting the most dangerous aspects of the

---

control. China and Russia must be firmly enlisted in a collaborative approach to controls, which means that hard decisions must be made about how far to push these states diplomatically and economically about other conflicting issues, such as how they treat their domestic populations (human rights) or reform their economies.[24] At the same time, decisions on how much military or militarily useful technology to share with such states cannot help but be affected somewhat by their internal stability.

It has been argued that arms transfers should be concentrated on states participating in international peacekeeping (the U.N. Security Council au-

international arms trade and reducing economic incentives to sell weapons abroad. ... The short-term goal of these talks should be to identify specifically prohibited transactions. The longer term goal should be to establish a dialogue between the suppliers and the recipients, and to lead to a comprehensive regime of conventional arms restraint under the auspices of the UN or some other regional fora.

6. Countries should recognize the possible link between the proliferation of advanced conventional weapons and the proliferation of weapons of mass destruction. For example, feared conventional force imbalances might lead some developing countries to pursue nuclear weapons as a deterrent. ... One option for curbing the flow of arms is to condition the sale of conventional arms upon the recipient's ratification of the Non-Proliferation Treaty.

7. The United States and other developed countries should actively support efforts by the World Bank and the International Monetary Fund to encourage member governments to reduce the size and cost of their armed forces, particularly by supporting programs to enhance transparency and accountability in the military sector and to demobilize troops and convert defense industries. They should also use their bilateral aid programs to achieve the same objectives.

8. The United States and other developed countries should continue to assist the former Soviet republics in developing effective export controls for conventional weapons.*

*The signatories included Nicole Hall, Overseas Development Council; Kathleen Bleakley, Arms Project of Human Rights Watch; William Durch, the Henry Stimson Center; Natalie Goldring, British American Security Information Council; William Hartung, World Policy Institute, New School for Social Research; William H. Kincade, American University; Michael Klare, Peace and World Security Studies Program, Five College Group (Amherst); Edward Laurance, Monterey Institute for International Studies; Lora Lumpe, Federation of American Scientists; Andrew Pierre, Carnegie Endowment for International Peace; Caleb Rossiter, Project on Demilitarization and Democracy; and Max Thelen, Jr.

SOURCE: Robbie Robbins, comp., "The Arms Trade in a Transitional Economy Conference Recommendations" (Palo Alto, CA: Global Outlook, 1993).

thorized its largest ever peacekeeping force, 28,000 troops, for the Somali turmoil, in 1993) or confined to weapons most suitable for defense (e.g., air defense missiles) rather than offense (e.g., long-range bombers). Yet we have seen that weapons themselves have no essentially offensive or defensive nature; anti-aircraft missiles are grave potential hazards if they wind up in the hands of terrorists aiming them at civilian airliners, whereas long-range bombers can be used for short-range defenses against massed troops. Helicopters can be used against an attacking enemy or a state's own population.

BOX 5.3 The Give and Take of Arms Transfer Controls

Pining for the lazy pace of the Cold War, when progress in arms control was measured in micrometers, and negotiators seemed to be talking about everything but cutting weapons? Welcome to the "Big 5" talks on arms sales, launched by President George Bush in the aftermath of the Gulf War.

After more than a year of talks, the major accomplishments of the world's largest weapons sellers—the United States, Russia, Britain, France, and China—remains two pages of vague and unenforceable guidelines for arms exports. ... The five produced "interim" principles on weapons of mass destruction, which a chief U.S. negotiator ... described as "completely non-binding stuff. ..."

The problem with the arms sales talks is the same as it was at the height of the Cold War: Everyone wants to look like they're talking about arms control, but nobody ... wants to cut weapons sales.

SOURCE: Lee Feinstein, "Arms R US," *Bulletin of the Atomic Scientists* 48 (November 1992): 8.

The key to arms restraint, therefore, is in the minds of decisionmakers and strategists. Defense, peacekeeping, or liberation doctrines that minimize destruction while preserving life, limb, and liberty must be fashioned. Those states grossly violating legal and humane principles and limits ought to be denied further armament if at all possible.

Sometimes, as in the former Yugoslavia of the 1990s, the right combination of defensive forces is unclear or infeasible because of such factors as terrain and the shortcomings and bullheadedness of political leaders. However, it might be feasible in such situations for IGOs such as NATO to place complete and enforced blockades and embargoes on any nearby nation facilitating arms, parts, or ammunition shipments to warring militias. My research has shown that concerted arms denials, especially when combined with other economic pressures, can gradually choke off fighting if parties are highly dependent.

Creative responses combining mass political movements or civil disobedience with prudent and appropriate force and arms diplomacy can at times be more effective than employment of superweapons. The best arms control system is still the human brain and conscience, a unique blend of high technology and ancient virtue, demonstrated, even against the will of political authorities, by the Oppenheimers and Sakharovs of this world.

Appendix   The 100 Largest Arms-Producing Firms in the OECD and Developing Countries, 1990 (figures in columns 6, 7, 8 and 10 in US $ million)

1	2	3	4	5	6	7	8	9	10	11
Rank[a]					Arms Sales		Total Sales	Col. 6 as	Profit	Employment
1990	1989[b]	Company[c]	Country	Industry	1990	1989[d]	1990	% of Col. 8	1990	1990
1	1	McDonnell Douglas	U.S.	Ac El Mi	9,020	8,890	16,255	55	306	121,200
2	2	General Dynamics	U.S.	Ac MV El Mi Sh	8,300	8,400	10,182	82	-578	98,100
3	5	British Aerospace	U.K.	Ac A El Mi SA/O	7,520	6,300	18,811	40	496	127,900
4	3	Lockheed	U.S.	Ac	7,500	7,400	9,958	75	335	73,000
S	4	General Motors	U.S.	Ac Eng El Mi	7,380	7,050	126,017	6	-1,986	761,400
S	S	Hughes Electronics (General Motors)	U.S.	Ac El	6,700	6,380	11,723	57	726	96,000
6	6	General Electric	U.S.	Ac Eng	6,450	6,250	58,414	11	4,303	298,000
7	7	Raytheon	U.S.	El Mi	5,500	5,330	9,632	57	557	76,700
S	S	Thomson-CSF (Thomson S.A.)	France	El Mi	5,250	4,120	6,799	77	399	46,900
8	12	Thomson S.A.	France	El Mi	5,250	4,320	13,811	38	-454	105,500
9	8	Boeing	U.S.	Ac El Mi	5,100	4,900	27,595	18	1,385	161,700
10	9	Northrop	U.S.	Ac	4,700	4,700	5,493	86	210	38,200
11	11	Martin Marietta	U.S.	Mi	4,600	4,350	6,143	75	328	62,000
12	18	GEC	U.K.	El	4,280	2,880	16,923	25	1,460	118,529
13	14	United Technologies	U.S.	Ac El Mi	4,100	4,100	21,442	19	751	192,600
14	10	Rockwell International	U.S.	Ac El Mi	4,100	4,500	12,443	33	624	101,900
15	13	Daimler Benz	FRG	Ac Eng MV El Sh	4,020	4,260	52,918	8	1,111	376,800
16	16	Direction des Constructions Navales	France	Sh	3,830	3,000	3,831	100	–	30,500
S	S	DASA (Daimler Benz)	FRG	Ac Eng El Mi	3,720	3,930	7,752	48	-84	61,276
17	20	Mitsubishi Heavy Industries	Japan	Ac MV Mi Sh	3,040	2,640	17,718	17	669	44,272
18	15	Litton Industries	U.S.	El Sh	3,000	3,000	5,156	58	179	50,600
19	17	TRW	U.S.	MV Oth	3,000	2,900	8,170	37	208	75,600
20	19	Grumman	U.S.	Ac El	2,900	2,850	4,014	72	86	26,100
21	25	Aérospatiale	France	Ac Mi	2,860	2,190	6,464	44	-73	37,691
22	23	IRI	Italy	Ac Eng El Sh	2,670	2,230	7,413	36	1	366,697

(continues)

Appendix (*continued*)

Rank[a]		Company[c]	Country	Industry	Arms Sales		Total Sales	Col. 6 as	Profit	Employment
1990	1989[b]				1990	1989[d]	1990	% of Col. 8	1990	1990
S	S	Pratt & Whitney (United Technologies)	U.S.	Eng	2,500	2,500	7,300	34	–	41,300
23	22	Westinghouse Electric	U.S.	EI	2,330	2,270	12,915	18	268	115,774
24	24	Dassault Aviation	France	Ac	2,260	2,200	3,454	65	52	14,900
25	26	Texas Instruments	U.S.	EI Mi Oth	2,120	2,160	6,567	32	-26	70,300
26	27	Tenneco	U.S.	Sh	2,110	1,950	14,511	15	561	92,000
S	S	Newport News (Tenneco)	U.S.	Sh	2,110	1,950	2,113	100	225	29,000
27	21	Unisys	U.S.	EI	2,000	2,300	10,111	20	-437	75,000
28	45	Loral	U.S.	EI	1,920	1,150	2,127	90	90	12,700
29	35	Textron	U.S.	Ac Eng MV	1,900	1,400	7,918	24	283	54,000
S	–	Alenia (IRI)	Italy	Ac EI Mi	1,840	0	3,069	60	25	21,981
30	44	Rolls Royce	U.K.	Eng	1,830	1,220	6,550	28	314	65,900
31	31	CEA Industrie	France	Oth	1,810	1,560	5,456	33	312	37,800
32	32	EFIM	Italy	Ac MV EI	1,710	1,510	2,178	79	-0	37,097
33	30	ITT	U.S.	EI	1,610	1,580	20,604	8	958	114,000
34	28	IBM	U.S.	EI Oth	1,600	1,600	69,018	2	6,020	373,816
35	38	INI	Spain	Ac A MV EI Sh SA/O	1,560	1,290	18,101	9	98	146,625
36	29	LTV	U.S.	Ac MV EI	1,490	1,580	6,138	24	71	35,300
37	41	SNECMA Groupe	France	Eng	1,490	1,260	4,322	34	38	27,616
38	49	GIAT Industries	France	A MV SA/O	1,430	1,020	1,469	97	–	15,000
39	37	Ordnance Factories	India	A SA/O Oth	1,430	1,400	1,468	97	–	–
S	S	MBB (DASA)	FRG	Ac EI Mi	1,420	1,840	2,853	50	37	23,229
40	42	E-Systems	U.S.	EI	1,350	1,250	1,810	75	86	18,435
41	34	Armscor	S. Africa	Ac A MV EI SA/O	1,330	1,460	1,663	80	–	18,900
42	33	Allied Signal	U.S.	Ac EI Oth	1,300	1,500	12,343	11	462	105,800
43	43	GTE	U.S.	EI	1,250	1,250	18,374	7	1,541	154,000
44	39	FIAT	Italy	Eng	1,180	1,280	7,145	17	2	303,238

Appendix (continued)

Rank 1990[a]	1989[b]	Company[c]	Country	Industry	Arms Sales 1990	Arms Sales 1989[d]	Total Sales 1990	Col. 6 as % of Col. 8	Profit 1990	Employment 1990
45	54	Matra Groupe	France	Mi El Oth	1,180	870	4,471	26	111	24,348
46	–	Alliant Tech Systems	U.S.	SA/O	1,150	0	1,248	92	24	8,000
47	48	Israel Aircraft Industries	Israel	Ac El Mi	1,120	1,030	1,400	80	13	16,650
S	S	MTU (DASA)	FRG	Eng	1,110	780	2,229	50	93	17,524
48	47	Oerlikon-Bührle	Switzerl.	Ac A El SA/O	1,080	1,040	3,375	32	-66	26,437
49	53	FMC	U.S.	MV Sh Oth	1,060	900	3,743	28	211	23,882
50	133	Bremer Vulkan	FRG	Sh	1,050	140	2,369	44	22	10,922
51	40	Kawasaki Heavy Industries	Japan	Ac Eng Sh	1,010	1,270	7,052	14	107	20,690
52	52	Siemens	FRG	El	990	900	39,107	3	1,032	373,000
53	50	Nobel Industries	Sweden	El Mi SA/O	930	950	4,606	20	199	26,654
54	55	VSEL Consortium	U.K.	MV Sh	930	870	933	100	-112	15,464
S	S	Matra Défense (Matra)	France	El Mi Oth	920	710	925	99	–	–
55	65	Diehl	FRG	A MV El SA/O	860	620	1,779	48	–	15,108
56	58	Hercules	U.S.	Ac Mi SA/O Oth	800	800	3,200	25	96	19,867
57	59	Harris	U.S.	El	790	800	3,052	26	131	33,400
58	51	Gencorp	U.S.	Ac Eng El Mi SA/O Oth	790	930	1,775	45	63	13,900
S	S	CASA (INI)	Spain	Ac	780	480	961	81	-39	10,050
S	S	Oto Melara (EFIM)	Italy	A MV Mi	780	580	783	100	4	2,245
59	80	Rheinmetall	FRG	A SA/O	750	510	1,838	41	58	14,062
60	73	Thyssen	FRG	MV Sh	710	540	22,396	3	427	149,644
61	66	Olin	U.S.	Ac El SA/O Oth	700	600	2,592	27	84	15,200
62	67	AT&T	U.S.	El	700	600	37,300	2	2,700	273,700
63	60	Sequa	U.S.	Eng El Oth	700	700	2,211	32	33	18,500
64	46	Ford Motor	U.S.	Ac MV El Mi	700	700	97,650	1	860	370,400
65	72	Eidgenössische Rüstungsbetriebe	Switzerl.	Ac Eng A SA/O	700	550	738	95	–	4,672

(continues)

Appendix (continued)

1	2	3	4	5	6	7	8	9	10	11
Rank[a]					Arms Sales		Total Sales	Col. 6 as	Profit	Employment
1990	1989[b]	Company[c]	Country	Industry	1990	1989[d]	1990	% of Col. 8	1990	1990
66	56	Mitsubishi Electric	Japan	El Mi	690	810	22,904	3	551	97,002
S	S	Telefunken System Technik (DASA)	FRG	El	680	730	1,045	65	44	9,372
S	S	SNECMA (SNECMA Groupe)	France	Eng	650	530	2,595	25	14	14,083
67	64	Motorola	U.S.	El	650	650	10,885	6	499	105,000
68	70	Israel Military Industries	Israel	A SA/O	640	590	655	98	−46	12,000
69	87	Lucas Industries	U.K.	Ac	630	490	4,221	15	149	54,942
70	62	Thiokol	U.S.	Eng Mi SA/O Oth	620	660	1,181	52	41	11,500
S	S	Bofors (Nobel Industries)	Sweden	A El Mi SA/O	620	740	657	94	–	4,549
71	61	Emerson Electric	U.S.	El	610	680	7,573	8	613	73,700
72	91	SAGEM Groupe	France	El	570	410	2,018	28	55	16,162
73	69	Science Applications Intl	U.S.	Ac Eng El	570	590	1,163	49	33	12,000
S	S	Agusta (EFIM)	Italy	Ac	560	610	927	60	−33	8,117
74	75	Computer Sciences	U.S.	El	560	530	1,738	32	65	23,000
75	71	Avondale Industries	U.S.	Sh	550	550	752	73	−26	8,500
S	S	AVCO (Textron)	U.S.	Ac	550	450	–	–	–	–
76	89	Ishikawajima-Harima	Japan	Eng Sh	540	460	6,677	8	137	15,280
77	82	Dassault Electronique	France	El	530	500	736	72	−8	4,331
78	95	Westland Group	U.K.	Ac	510	390	734	69	76	9,800
79	79	FFV	Sweden	A El SA/O Oth	500	510	1,055	47	–	9,709
S	S	Dornier (DASA)	FRG	Ac El Mi	500	590	1,787	28	−23	10,931
80	84	Teledyne	U.S.	Eng El Mi	500	500	3,446	15	95	33,200
81	77	Hindustan Aeronautics	India	Ac Mi	500	520	515	97	23	43,000
82	68	Smiths Industries	U.K.	El	490	590	1,201	41	161	13,100
S	S	Hollandse Signaal (Thomson-CSF)	Netherl.	El	490	330	515	95	−46	4,522
83	85	Racal Electronics	U.K.	El	480	490	3,719	13	257	38,461

Appendix (continued)

1	2	3	4	5	6	7	8	9	10	11
Rank[a]					Arms Sales		Total Sales	Col. 6 as	Profit	Employment
1990	1989[b]	Company[c]	Country	Industry	1990	1989[d]	1990	% of Col. 8	1990	1990
84	100	Hawker Siddeley	U.K.	El	480	350	3,887	12	145	44,600
S	–	Systemtechnik Nord (Bremer Vulkan)	FRG	El	470	0	629	75	–1	2,397
85	92	Devonport Management	U.K.	Sh	470	410	500	94	15	7,942
S	S	EN Bazan (INI)	Spain	Sh	460	300	530	87	29	9,613
S	S	FIAT Aviazione (FIAT)	Italy	Ac Eng	460	410	841	55	21	4,666
86	76	SAAB-SCANIA	Sweden	Ac Eng	450	530	5,339	8	60	32,536
87	93	Dowty Group	U.K.	Ac El	450	400	1,372	33	1	15,022
88	74	Thorn EMI	U.K.	El	450	540	6,532	7	462	57,932
89	88	Ferranti-International Signal	U.K.	El	440	470	817	54	–175	10,325
90	63	Hunting	U.K.	SA/O	420	650	1,377	31	69	6,918
91	78	Rafael	Israel	SA/O Oth	420	510	420	100	–17	5,960
92	99	Mannesmann	FRG	MV	410	360	14,819	3	287	124,000
S	S	Krauss-Maffei (Mannesmann)	FRG	MV	410	360	873	47	14	5,408
93	83	Toshiba	Japan	El Mi	410	500	32,429	1	835	162,000
S	S	Sextant Avion (Thomson-CSF/ Aérospatiale)	France	El	400	350	1,119	36	35	9,152
S	S	Collins International (Rockwell International)	U.S.	El	400	300	–	–	–	–
S	S	CFM Intern (General Electric & SNECMA)	U.S.	Ac Eng	400	500	–	–	–	–
94	105	Lürssen	FRG	Sh	400	320	495	81	–	1,080
S	–	Esco Electronics (Emerson Electric)	U.S.	El	400	0	–	–	–	6,100
S	S	SAGEM (SAGEM Groupe)	France	El	390	280	946	41	27	6,392
95	90	Sundstrand	U.S.	Ac	390	430	1,600	24	114	13,000
96	81	NEC	Japan	El	380	510	25,546	1	376	117,994
97	97	Morrison Knudsen	U.S.	MV Oth	380	380	1,653	23	35	–

Appendix (continued)

1	2	3	4	5	6	7	8	9	10	11
Rank^a					Arms Sales		Total Sales 1990	Col. 6 as % of Col. 8	Profit 1990	Employment 1990
1990	1989^b	Company^c	Country	Industry	1990	1989^d				
98	101	Mitre	U.S.	EI	370	350	–	–	–	–
99	102	Dyncorp	U.S.	Ac EI	360	350	717	50	–	18,000
100	36	Honeywell	U.S.	EI Mi	360	1,400	6,309	6	382	60,300

– Data not available.

^aBoth the rank designation and the arms sales figures for 1989 are also given, in columns 2 and 7, respectively, for comparison with the data for 1990 in columns 1 and 6.

^bThe rank designation in this column may not correspond to that given in table 8A in the SIPRI Yearbook 1991. A dash (–) in this column indicates either that the company did not produce arms in 1989, in which case there is a zero (0) in column 7, or that it did not rank among the 100 largest companies in table 8A in the SIPRI Yearbook 1991, in which case figures for arms sales in 1989 do appear in column 7. A figure above 100 in this column shows the actual rank order in 1989, although the company was not included in the SIPRI 100 table in the SIPRI Yearbook 1991.

^cCompany names in parentheses after the name of the ranked company are the names of the holding companies. The parent companies, with data pertaining to them, appear in their rank order for 1990. Profits are taken for company as whole, not just arms sector.

^dA zero (0) in this column indicates that the company did not produce arms in 1989, but began arms production in 1990, or that in 1989 the company did not exist as it was structured in 1990.

ABBREVIATIONS: A = artillery, Ac = aircraft, EI = electronics, Eng = engines, Mi = missiles, MV = military vehicles, SA/O = small arms/ordnance, Sh = ships, Oth = other.

SOURCE: SIPRI Yearbook 1992: World Armaments and Disarmament (Oxford: Oxford University Press, 1992), pp. 392–397.

□ □ □

Discussion Questions

CHAPTER ONE

1. Some say that the use of arms today has changed little from ancient times; others point to revolutionary changes. Which view is closer to the truth?

2. Which are the best predictors of the types of weapons seen in any particular era: that era's level of artistic development, level of religious or moral development, level of warfare, or level of science and technology?

3. Name some effects that weapons have in addition to their specific impacts on battles. Name some effects often associated with weapons that may be mistaken or exaggerated.

4. Describe what might be called the traditional hierarchy of access to weapons among nations in the world.

5. Is it correct to say that the global spread of arms has been uniform and rapid since 1648? Explain your answer.

6. What accounts for the lowering of arms supply and demand in world politics for the past several years?

7. Is the number of states importing large amounts of weapons very great in today's world? What factors characterize the major arms customers?

8. What gives major powers the market advantage in the sale of arms as compared to smaller suppliers?

9. What are the main trends signaling the future of the arms trade? What are the main implications of higher-tech weapons?

10. Judging from the arms proliferation trends noted in this chapter, what should be the primary concerns of those wishing to limit the arms trade? Is arms proliferation likely to get out of control soon?

CHAPTER TWO

1. Would you characterize the spread of (a) arms and (b) arms technologies in today's world as rapid or slow? What factors influence that pace?

2. Describe the general relationships between companies and governments in the arms business. What are the benefits that firms see in exporting arms? What are the benefits that governments see? Is it accurate to characterize the arms business as "the most socialized part of capitalist economies"?

3. Is it correct to say that arms manufacturers generally seek to supply only their own country's armed forces? Explain your answer.

4. Do major power governments generally encourage a "free for all" in arms exports with very few restrictions or regulations attached? Why or why not?

5. Are bureaucracies noted for devising revolutionary new approaches to acquiring and using weapons? Cite reasons and examples.

6. How do breakthroughs in military technology affect both a state's security and its welfare?

7. Cite some ways by which the security, alternatives, and political dilemmas apply to the manufacture of arms. Should governments attempt to control scientific research that might lead to very destructive or destabilizing arms?

8. Arms production has been called nearly irresistible or addictive for states. Yet some, such as Japan, have deemphasized production or concentrated only on limited aspects of it. What has led such states to resist the lure of a weapons economy? What are some of the economic arguments for and against arms manufacture?

9. Do states new to the weapons production business enjoy conspicuous advantages over long-established arms producers? Explain your answer.

10. Is the predominant pattern of armament in today's world labor intensive/self-reliant, capital intensive/dependent, labor intensive/dependent, or capital intensive/self-reliant? What are the implications of this pattern?

CHAPTER THREE

1. In what ways might arms transfers be a mechanism of influence for the supplier over the recipient government? How reliable is that influence likely to be?

2. Is it true that a country's military usually tends to favor supplying arms to other friendly states? Why or why not?

3. What factors stand in the way of effective restrictions on the export of arms?

4. Cite some areas of major power agreement in controlling the spread of arms.

5. What is the prevailing evidence about the causation dilemma?

6. What distinguishes the black from the gray market for weapons? Why do governments, even those that sometimes engage in these markets, fear them?

7. What are the main channels for the black and gray trade in arms? What recent trends are detectable in the amount of each type?

8. If someone proposed arming the victims of aggression in world politics, how would you respond? What are the pros and cons of doing so?

9. What seems to have been the relative impact of arms embargoes and arms shipments during recent wars?

10. In what ways do different regions differ in their pattern of arms importation?

CHAPTER FOUR

1. What were some of the reasons for the failure of past U.S. arms transfer control efforts?

2. Which approach seems to best typify the arms transfer policies of major powers: unlimited sales, strict prohibitions, case-by-case determinations, or sales

only to the most trustworthy allies? Explain why the major powers prefer this particular approach.

3. Name the factors that historically have tended to characterize successful and unsuccessful arms control or disarmament agreements. What was the first multilateral agreement to address the international arms trade?

4. Is it correct to say that disarmament attempts have gone out of style in the twentieth century? Explain your answer.

5. What steps have been taken to remedy problems of either horizontal or vertical arms proliferation?

6. Detail the role or value of verification in arms control processes.

7. Why are political interests fundamental to arms control agreements? Give some examples.

8. Which psychological and political factors are fundamental to controlling weapons spread?

9. Cite some pros and cons of defense conversion.

10. Which of the approaches and principles for controlling the spread of weapons seem most feasible, either politically or economically?

CHAPTER FIVE

1. Cite elements of change, continuity, and new challenges for arms control in the developing weapons picture in world politics.

2. Some people have argued that arms races do not cause wars. Do you agree? In what ways might arms acquisition be said either to contribute to or ease rising tensions and a warlike atmosphere?

3. Which arms trade trend is *not* illustrated by recent India-Pakistan competition: purchase of weapons upgrades, acquisition of higher technologies, substantially reduced defense budgets, nuclear proliferation, or confidence-building measures?

4. What are future weapons likely to look like and with what implications for budgets, deterrence, and arms control?

5. When arms are shipped to besieged parties in war, what are some of the possible outcomes? What might policymakers want to know about a crisis in deciding whether to ship arms to the parties?

6. Is it fair for customer governments to demand offsets and countertrade from countries selling them arms? Does this undermine a traditional pattern of free trade and free markets in arms?

7. How do changes in the international system affect the global distribution of weapons and related technology?

8. What are some of the main remedies being proposed for arms transfer dilemmas?

9. What are some shortcomings of these remedies?

10. Who should be armed in world politics and to what extent?

□ □ □

Notes

INTRODUCTION

1. Nadav Safran, *From War to War: The Arab-Israeli Confrontation, 1948–67* (New York: Pegasus, 1969).

CHAPTER ONE

1. Keith Krause, *Arms and the State: Patterns of Military Production and Trade* (Cambridge: Cambridge University Press, 1992), p. 1.

2. Ibid., p. 1.

3. Martin Van Creveld, *Technology and War: From 2000 B.C. to the Present* (New York: Free Press, 1989), pp. 14–15.

4. Russell Warren Howe, *Weapons: The International Game of Arms, Money, and Diplomacy* (Garden City, NY: Doubleday, 1980), p. 14.

5. See N. Chagnon, *Yanomamo: The Fierce People,* 3d ed. (New York: Holt, Rinehart, and Winston, 1983); Morton Fried, Marvin Harris, and Robert Murphy, eds., *War: The Anthropology of Armed Conflict and Aggression* (Garden City, NY: Natural History Press, 1968); Van Creveld, op. cit., p. 21.

6. Robert L. O'Connell, *Of Arms and Men: A History of War, Weapons, and Aggression* (Oxford: Oxford University Press, 1989), p. 189.

7. Ibid., p. 171.

8. Ibid., pp. 189–190.

9. Van Creveld, op. cit., Ch. 5.

10. Daniel Patrick Moynihan, quoted November 1993.

11. Krause, op. cit., Chs. 1–3.

12. Howe, op. cit., p. 316.

13. Michael Barnett and Alexander Wendt, "The Systemic Sources of Dependent Militarization," in *Insecurity Dilemma: National Security of Third World States,* ed. Brian L. Job (Boulder: Lynne Rienner, 1992), pp. 97–119.

14. Krause, op. cit., pp. 34–43.

15. Ralph Sanders, *Arms Industries: New Suppliers and Regional Security* (Washington, DC: National Defense University Press, 1990), p. 8.

16. Krause, op. cit., Ch. 3.

17. Barnett and Wendt, op. cit., p. 106.

18. O'Connell, op. cit., pp. 194–195.

19. Ibid.

20. Krause, op. cit., Ch. 3.

21. Sanders, op. cit., p. 9.

22. As early as the nineteenth century, certain newly industrializing states, such as Egypt under its modernizing ruler Muhammad Ali, had progressed fairly far in developing indigenous military production, only to have major powers intervene to dismantle the emerging state-owned arms factories in the name of economic efficiency, "free trade," and repayment of debts (a set of priorities echoed today in International Monetary Fund demands for Third World economic reform). See Barnett and Wendt, op. cit., p. 107.

23. Robert E. Harkavy, "The Changing International System and the Arms Trade" (Paper presented at the Workshop on Arms Trade and Arms Control in the Post–Cold War World: Future Trends and Developments, Center for War/Peace Studies, Columbia University, New York, November 1993), pp. 26–27.

24. Barnett and Wendt, op. cit., pp. 114–117.

25. Ian Anthony et al., "The Trade in Major Conventional Weapons," in *SIPRI Yearbook 1991: World Armaments and Disarmament* (Oxford: Oxford University Press, 1991), p. 197. See also Keith Krause and Stephanie G. Neuman commentary at Workshop on Arms Trade; and Ian Anthony, Paul Claesson, Elisabeth Sköns, and Siemon T. Wezeman, "Arms Production and Trade," in *SIPRI Yearbook 1993: World Armaments and Disarmament* (Oxford: Oxford University Press, 1993), p. 416.

26. See Federation of American Scientists, *Arms Sales Monitor*, no. 16 (June-July 1992): 6; Eric Schmidt, "Arms Sales to Third World, Especially by Russians, Drop," *New York Times*, July 20, 1993. One must be aware that arms trade estimates can vary from source to source because of varying definitions, focus on different types of weapons, government secrecy, and different dates for agreements and deliveries. It is therefore best to compare numerous data sources.

27. Giovanni de Briganti, "Government Stance Riles French Firms," *Defense News*, June 28–July 4, 1993, p. 1.

28. Herbert Wulf, "Arms Industry Limited: The Turning Point in the 1990s," in *Arms Industry Limited*, ed. Herbert Wulf (Oxford: Oxford University Press, 1993), p. 8.

29. *National Geographic* (March 1993). See also Krause and Neuman commentary at Workshop on Arms Trade.

30. Daniel Sneider, "Russians Extol Fighter Sale," *Defense News*, July 5–11, 1993, p. 1.

31. See Michael Collins Dunn, "At the 'End of History,' the Arms Bazaar Becomes a Yard Sale," *Washington Post Report on Middle East Affairs* 13 (August-September 1992): 20.

32. Federation of American Scientists, *Arms Sales Monitor*, no. 21 (July 1993): 1.

33. Anthony, Claesson, Sköns, and Wezeman, op. cit., p. 417. On the Middle East's continued import potential, see Philip Finnegan, "Middle East Arms Sales Won't Drop," *Defense News*, September 20–26, 1993, p. 3.

34. Anthony, Claesson, Sköns, and Wezeman, op. cit., Tables 10.10, 10.11.

35. On the still-unresolved debate about whether arms spending helps or hinders an economy, see Stephanie G. Neuman, "The Defense Sector and Economic Development: A Survey and Debate" (Paper presented at Workshop on Arms Trade).

36. Anthony et al., op. cit., pp. 197–199.

37. Robert E. Harkavy, "The Changing International System and the Arms Trade" (Paper presented at Workshop on Arms Trade), p. 33.

38. Anthony et al., op. cit., pp. 198–199.

39. Ibid., p. 205.

40. Ibid., pp. 201–203.

41. Observation by Dov Zakheim at Workshop on Arms Trade. See also Patrick E. Tyler, "Russia and China in Military Pact: Technology Transfer Seen as Aim," *New York Times*, November 10, 1993.

42. Dunn, op. cit., p. 20.

43. International Institute for Strategic Studies, *Military Balance: 1985–1986* (London: IISS, 1985).

44. See Christian Catrina, *Arms Transfers and Dependence* (New York: Taylor and Francis/UNIDIR, 1988), p. 29. Stephanie Neuman has supported such contentions with commentary at various conferences of the International Studies Association.

45. Witness the prolonged delays in bringing out Europe's fighter aircraft of the next century, the Euro-fighter, to be built by a multinational team of companies. One major sticking point has been finding a capable enough European computer to handle the "fly by wire" requirements of the electronic cockpit controls. Thus, ironically in seeking a more multinational defense industry, elements of nationalism, in this case Euro-nationalism, are still built in so that equipment from other regions, such as Japan or the United States, is excluded. See also Western European Union Assembly, *Defence Industry in Spain and Portugal*, Doc. 1161 (Brussels: Western European Union, November 7, 1988), p. 9.

46. Wulf, op. cit., pp. 6–7.

47. East Germany also marketed counterfeit ammunition for West German infantry weapons, even offering to stamp the correct West German weapons arsenal on the shells. Such imitations, which also came from China, did not always fit or fire properly, but they were cheap and readily available. Alternatives such as these have been a military lifeline when a key supplier could not or would not deliver required spare parts or when costs mounted.

48. Patrick Brogan, *Deadly Business: Sam Cummings, Interarms, and the Arms Trade* (New York: Norton, 1983).

49. Frederic S. Pearson, Michael Brzoska, and Christer Crantz, "The Effects of Arms Transfers on Wars and Peace Negotiations," in *SIPRI Yearbook 1992: World Armaments and Disarmament* (Oxford: Oxford University Press, 1992), Ch. 10.

50. Neuman, op. cit., p. 35.

CHAPTER TWO

1. See Stockholm International Peace Research Institute, *Arms Uncontrolled* (Cambridge, MA: Harvard University Press, 1975).

2. Attempts to measure the defense spending burden of LDCs are particularly plagued by faulty data; much economic activity in these countries goes unreported, which probably makes the proportion of the gross national product spent on the military at times seem higher than it is. Third World diplomats and writers have denied that their defense spending proportionally rivals that of the major

powers. Yet although global military spending has been concentrated among the more industrialized countries, it has been growing faster among many of the most ambitious LDCs—prominent among them, India, China, Egypt, Brazil, Iran, Iraq, Pakistan, and Indonesia, which, not coincidentally, have launched major programs to acquire and produce advanced weaponry. Analysts also point to a trade-off between devoting scarce resources to military buildups and realizing the potential for economic development. The Chinese government, for one however, appears to believe in the possibility of dual modernizations, of having both guns and butter. See Keith Krause, "Arms Imports, Arms Production, and the Quest for Security in the Third World," in *The Insecurity Dilemma: National Security of Third World States*, ed. Brian L. Job (Boulder: Lynne Rienner, 1992), pp. 121–130; Herbert Wulf, "Arms Industry Limited: The Turning Point in the 1990s," in *Arms Industry Limited*, ed. Herbert Wulf (Oxford: Oxford University Press/SIPRI, 1993), p. 9; James L. Payne, *Why Nations Arm* (Oxford: Basil Blackwell, 1989), pp. 14–15, Ch. 15.

3. Payne, op. cit., p. 38.

4. Krause, op. cit., p. 134.

5. Payne, op. cit., Ch. 4, pp. 177–178. See also Frederic S. Pearson, "The Correlates of Arms Importation," *Journal of Peace Research* 26, no. 2 (1989): 153–163.

6. See advertisements in publications such as *Aviation Week and Space Technology; Defense News; Jane's Defence Weekly; Defence and Diplomacy;* and Royal United Services Institute for Defence Studies, RUSI, *RUSI and Brassey's Defence Yearbook*.

7. See Herbert Wulf, "Arms Production," in *SIPRI Yearbook 1991: World Armaments and Disarmament* (Oxford: Oxford University Press, 1991), Ch. 8.

8. Richard Boudreaux, "Russian Defense Industry Adopts Capitalist Strategy," *Los Angeles Times*, February 12, 1993.

9. Keith Krause, *Arms and the State: Patterns of Military Production and Trade* (Cambridge: Cambridge University Press, 1992), Ch. 3.

10. Russell Warren Howe, *Weapons: The International Game of Arms, Money, and Diplomacy* (Garden City, NY: Doubleday, 1980), p. 317.

11. Ibid., pp. 318–319.

12. Ibid., p. 319; George Thayer, *The War Business: The International Trade in Armaments* (New York: Clarion, 1969), pp. 305–307.

13. Michael Barnett and Alexander Wendt, "The Systemic Sources of Dependent Militarization," in *The Insecurity Dilemma*, pp. 108–109. Not only are most arms industries nationalized in NICs, but often there is only one firm that can produce a specific weapon. Almost no competition exists among defense firms in LDCs. However, some NICs have accepted bids from foreign arms producers, thus stimulating competition for domestic industries. See Ralph Sanders, *Arms Industries: New Suppliers and Regional Security* (Washington, DC: National Defense University Press, 1990), p. 8.

14. Howe, op. cit., pp. 325–327, Ch. 5.

15. Wulf, "Arms Production," pp. 285–286. The breakup and economic reform of the former Eastern bloc should bring additional major producers to the open market, thus further depressing prices and cutting into profits, unless profitable multinational deals can be struck among them for cheaper labor or expanded markets. Another ranking of defense firms for 1992 showed that twenty-six of the

thirty-nine largest firms were American, accounting for roughly twice the level of defense sales as the ten leading European firms. See Philip Finnegan, "U.S. Firms Find Profit in Worldwide Consolidation," *Defense News*, July 19–25, 1993, pp. 1, 8.

16. Boudreaux, op. cit. See also Wulf, "Arms Production," p. 286.

17. Elizabeth Sköns and Herbert Wulf, "The Internationalization of the Arms Industry" (Paper presented at the Workshop on Arms Trade and Arms Control in the Post–Cold War World: Future Trends and Developments, Center for War/Peace Studies, Columbia University, New York, November 1993).

18. See, for example, Mark A. Lorell, *Multinational Development of Large Aircraft* (Santa Monica, CA: Rand, 1980).

19. These partnerships must take account of emerging trade groups or blocs, such as the EC, that can create barriers to outside firms. Other blocs or alliances, such as NATO, offer ways around these barriers for alliance leaders such as the United States, which gain an admission ticket to compete for defense sales in the alliance "club." At least through the 1990s, the EC itself had only limited powers in defense and security and hence limited effects on such sales.

20. See Seymour Melman, *Pentagon Capitalism: The Political Economy of War* (New York: McGraw-Hill, 1970); and the work of Marion Anderson, Employment Research Associates, Lansing, MI, including *The Empty Pork Barrel: Unemployment and the Pentagon Budget* (Lansing: Pilgrim, 1978).

21. Steven Chan commentary at Workshop on Arms Trade.

22. Edward A. Kolodziej and Frederic S. Pearson, "The Political Economy of Making and Marketing Arms: A Test for the Systemic Imperatives of Order and Welfare," *Occasional Papers*, no. 8904 (St. Louis: Center for International Studies, University of Missouri–St. Louis, April 1989), p. 5.

23. See Graham Allison, *Essence of Decision: Explaining the Cuban Missile Crisis* (Boston: Little, Brown, 1971).

24. See Edward L. Katzenbach, "The Horse Cavalry in the Twentieth Century: A Study in Policy Response," and Warner R. Schilling, "The H-Bomb Decision: How to Decide Without Actually Choosing," in *Readings in American Foreign Policy: A Bureaucratic Perspective*, ed. Morton H. Halperin and Arnold Kanter (Boston: Little, Brown, 1973), Part II.

25. See, for example, Nazli Choucri and Robert C. North, *Nations in Conflict: National Growth and International Violence* (San Francisco: Freeman, 1975), pp. 203–218.

26. Pearson, op. cit., pp. 153–163.

27. Karl von Clausewitz, *On War*, ed. by Anatol Rapoport (Baltimore: Penguin, 1968).

28. See Martin Van Creveld, *Technology and War: From 2000 B.C. to the Present* (New York: Free Press, 1989), pp. 219–222.

29. Ultimately, Oppenheimer would campaign unsuccessfully with the Eisenhower administration against development of fusion weapons—what came to be called hydrogen bombs. As a result, he was labeled a security risk by the very government that had sponsored his research. The Manhattan Project is graphically described in the documentary film *The Day After Trinity*. Ironically, the father of the Soviet fusion weapon, Andrei Sakharov, was later branded an enemy of the Soviet

state and sent to an insane asylum when he too raised political objections to the bomb.

30. Edward A. Kolodziej, *Making and Marketing Arms: The French Experience and Its Implications for the International System* (Princeton: Princeton University Press, 1987); Kolodziej and Pearson, op. cit.

31. Controversy exists among experts about whether and to what extent these action-reaction sequences exist; see, for example, Payne, op. cit., pp. 69–81.

32. *Le Monde*, October 20, 1988, p. 4. For an overview of findings regarding these possibilities, see Steve Chan, "The Impact of Defense Spending on Economic Performance: A Survey of Evidence and Problems," *Orbis* 29 (Summer 1985): 403–434; Nicole Ball, *Security and Economy in the Third World* (Princeton: Princeton University Press, 1988); Saadet Deger, *Military Expenditure in Third World Countries: The Economic Effects* (London: Routledge and Kegan Paul, 1986). On Japan's defense industry, see Naoaki Usui, "Diversification Shields Japanese Defense Firms," *Defense News*, July 19–25, 1993, p. 14.

33. William Perry and Juan Carlos Weiss, "Brazil," in *Sowing the Dragon's Teeth: The Implications of Third World Military Industrialization*, ed. James E. Katz (Lexington, MA: Lexington Books, 1986).

34. Raju G.C. Thomas, *Indian Security Policy* (Princeton: Princeton University Press, 1987), pp. 195–274; S. Hazarika, "India Plans to Increase Imports and Exports," *New York Times*, February 5, 1989.

35. Robert M. Cutler, Laure Depres, and Aaron Karp, "The Political-Economy of East-South Military Transfers," *International Studies Quarterly* 41 (September 1987): 291.

36. Barnett and Wendt, op. cit., Ch. 5.

CHAPTER THREE

1. See Arthur Jay Klinghofer, with Judith Apter, *Israel and the Soviet Union: Alienation or Reconciliation?* (Boulder: Westview, 1985), p. 123.

2. Stockholm International Peace Research Institute, *The Arms Trade with the Third World* (Stockholm: Almqvist and Wiksell, 1971).

3. Andrew Pierre, *The Global Politics of Arms Sales* (Princeton: Princeton University Press, 1982).

4. John Sislin, "The Elusive Link Between Military Assistance and Political Compliance" (Ph.D. diss., Indiana University–Bloomington, 1993). See also Keith Krause, *Arms and the State: Patterns of Military Production and Trade* (Cambridge: Cambridge University Press, 1992), pp. 198–215; and Christian Catrina, *Arms Transfers and Dependence* (New York: Taylor and Francis/UNIDIR, 1988), Ch. 4, Part II.

5. See Michael Brzoska and Frederic S. Pearson, *Arms and Warfare: Escalation, De-escalation, Negotiation* (Columbia: University of South Carolina Press, 1994).

6. Federation of American Scientists, *Arms Sales Monitor*, no. 16 (June-July 1992). A bit later the Clinton administration decided to continue this policy of promoting defense exports but also to restrict use of U.S. foreign aid in commercial sales, mainly because of some cases of fraud. See David Silverberg, "U.S. FMF Restraints Rattle Israel," *Defense News*, June 21–27, 1993, pp. 4, 28.

7. Paul Leventhal and Daniel Horner, "Bush's Voodoo Non-proliferation," *Christian Science Monitor*, July 20, 1992.

8. "Illegal and Covert Arms Transfers" (Washington, DC: Center for Defense Information, August 30, 1993), p. 1.

9. Ibid., p. 1. See also Aaron Karp, "The Black and Grey Markets" (Paper presented at the Workshop on Arms Trade and Arms Control in the Post–Cold War World: Future Trends and Developments, Center for War/Peace Studies, Columbia University, New York, November 1993).

10. Michael Klare commentary at ibid.

11. "Illegal and Covert Arms Transfers."

12. See Michael Intrilligator and Dagobert L. Brito, "Can Arms Races Lead to the Outbreak of War?" *Journal of Conflict Resolution* 28 (March 1984): 63–84; George W. Downs, David M. Rockes, and Randolph M. Siverson, "Arms Races and Cooperation," *World Politics* 38 (October 1985): 188–246; Michael D. Wallace, "Armaments and Escalation: Two Competing Hypotheses," *International Studies Quarterly* 26 (March 1982): 37–56; Michael D. Wallace, "Arms Races and Escalation: Some New Evidence," *Journal of Conflict Resolution* 23 (March 1979): 3–16.

13. Curt Gasteyger, *Searching for World Security: Understanding Global Armament and Disarmament* (London: Frances Pinter, 1985), p. 11.

14. Geoffrey Blainey, *The Causes of War*, 3d ed. (Basingstoke: Macmillan, 1988); Bruce Bueno de Mesquita, *The War Trap* (New Haven: Yale University Press, 1981).

15. "El Salvador 'Invasion' of Honduras," p. A1, and "New Clash on Honduran Border," p. A4, *Times* (London), July 15, 1969; H. J. Maidenberg, "New Clashes Mar Latin Cease-fire," *New York Times*, July 18, 1969, p. A1.

16. See Gene Sharp, *Civilian-Based Defense: A Post-Military Weapons System* (Princeton: Princeton University Press, 1990).

17. Keith Krause, "Arms Imports, Arms Production, and the Quest for Security in the Third World," in *The Insecurity Dilemma: National Security of Third World States*, ed. Brian L. Job (Boulder: Lynne Rienner, 1992), p. 127.

18. Ibid., pp. 127–128. See also Krause commentary at Workshop on Arms Trade.

19. Krause, "Arms Imports," p. 127.

20. Frederic S. Pearson, Michael Brzoska, and Christer Crantz, "The Effects of Arms Transfers on Wars and Peace Negotiations," in *SIPRI Yearbook 1992: World Armaments and Disarmament* (Oxford: Oxford University Press, 1992), Ch. 10. These findings are further elaborated in Brzoska and Pearson, op. cit.

21. Pearson, Brzoska, and Crantz, op. cit., p. 415.

22. Krause, "Arms Imports," pp. 129–130.

23. Brzoska and Pearson, op. cit., Ch. 5.

CHAPTER FOUR

1. Richard Burt, *Arms Control in the 1980s* (Boulder: Westview, 1984).

2. Subsequently, although reporting took place and some deals were withdrawn or revised, no major agreements actually were vetoed.

3. Frederic S. Pearson, "U.S. Arms Transfer Policy: The Feasibility of Restraint," *Arms Control* 2 (May 1981): 25–65.

4. Ibid., pp. 30–33.

5. U.S. Department of State, "Review of Arms Transfer Policy," *Current Policy,* no. 145 (Washington, DC: March 6, 1980), p. 2.

6. Frederic S. Pearson, "The Question of Control in British Defence Sales Policy," *International Affairs* 59 (Spring 1983): 223–228.

7. Frederic S. Pearson, "'Necessary Evil': Perspectives on West German Arms Transfer Policies," *Armed Forces and Society* 12 (Summer 1986): 531–533.

8. Christopher J. Lamb, *How to Think About Arms Control, Disarmament, and Defense* (Englewood Cliffs, NJ: Prentice-Hall, 1988), p. 11.

9. Ibid., pp. 21–22.

10. Today, Japan's defense budget nominally is limited to about 1 percent of GNP, for example, but Japan's GNP is large enough to afford the country one of Asia's largest armed forces and arms-related industries.

11. Lamb, op. cit., pp. 21–22. One might cite Costa Rica's elimination of its army in the 1950s as an example of unilateral disarmament; it was designed as much to avoid domestic coups as to reassure neighbors of Costa Rica's peaceful intent. Yet the country still retains armed border and police units.

12. Charles E. Osgood, *An Alternative to War or Surrender?* (Urbana: University of Illinois Press, 1962); "Questioning Some Unquestioned Assumptions About National Defense," *Journal of Arms Control* 1 (January 1963): 2–13.

13. Lamb, op. cit., p. 44.

14. Ibid., pp. 22–25. See also Robert L. O'Connell, *Of Arms and Men: A History of War, Weapons, and Aggression* (Oxford: Oxford University Press, 1989), p. 272.

15. David G. Anderson, "The International Arms Trade: Regulating Conventional Arms Transfers in the Aftermath of the Gulf War," *American University Journal of International Law and Policy* 7 (Summer 1992): 760.

16. Ibid., pp. 761–762.

17. Lamb, op. cit., p. 49.

18. These include the U.S. executive and congressional branches, both of which publish data (see the U.S. Arms Control and Disarmament and Congressional Research Service publications); private scholarly institutes (such as the International Institute for Strategic Studies [IISS] in London and the Stockholm International Peace Research Institute [SIPRI] in Sweden); and military publications (such as *Jane's Defence Weekly* and *Aviation Week,* which publish arms transfer chronologies or summaries).

Even though much useful data are published, each source has its own definitions of what to count and its own methods of gaining information. Totals therefore vary and never fully describe all commercial and covert dealings; yet they generally show similar basic trends. Until the United Nations can provide a comprehensive and widely agreed reporting format, it is important to use multiple data sources. Adequate arms transfer measurements would have to cover (1) "excessive accumulation" of weapons, (2) the spread of advanced arms technology, (3) trends in small arms transfers, (4) flows of arms financing, (5) transfer of licenses, (6) transfer of components and finished weapons systems, and (7) covert arms flow. This is a major challenge for the United Nations or any data-gathering agencies. See Ian Anthony, "Current Trends and Developments in the Arms

Trade" (Paper presented at the Workshop on Arms Trade and Arms Control in the Post–Cold War World: Future Trends and Developments, Center for War/Peace Studies, Columbia University, New York, 1993).

19. Lamb, op. cit., pp. 43–44.

20. Anderson, op. cit., p. 767.

21. See Paul Lewis, "U.S. Urges China to Pressure North Koreans to Open Nuclear Sites," *New York Times*, February 5, 1994.

22. Ian Bellany and Coit D. Blacker, eds., *The Verification of Arms Control Agreements* (London: Frank Cass, 1983).

23. See Lamb, op. cit., pp. 45–46.

24. Study by the Rand Corporation, cited on National Public Radio, November 18, 1993.

25. Amy Smithson, quoted by Peter Grier, "Chemical Arms Draft Took 20 Years—Now Comes the Hard Part," *Christian Science Monitor*, October 20, 1992.

26. National Public Radio, January 13, 1993.

27. Allan S. Krass, "Death and Transfiguration: Nuclear Arms Control in the 1980s and 1990s," in *World Security: Trends and Challenges at Century's End*, ed. Michael T. Klare and Daniel C. Thomas (New York: St. Martin's, 1991), pp. 80–93. On the issue of space weapons, U.S.-Soviet frictions over Strategic Defense Initiative research in the 1980s became a basically moot point when budget pressures forced cancellation of the program in the early 1990s. The Outer Space Treaty of 1969 is meant to ban offensive or mass destructive weapons in space. Yet it does not cover suborbital systems in space, such as missiles, devices that are not placed in sustained orbit or on celestial bodies (e.g., the moon). Some antisatellite (ASAT) weapons that would knock out an opponent's "eyes and ears" in space—that is, communications and intelligence ("spy") satellites—also would not necessarily be banned in the treaty. Informally, a congressional refusal to fund research and a unilateral Soviet moratorium halted the ASAT race in the 1980s, but no formal agreements were signed.

28. O'Connell, op. cit., p. 272.

29. Associated with the main regimes outlined in Table 4.1 are secondary ones as well: a supercomputer control agreement among prime manufacturing states, the United States, and Japan; measures to discourage scientists in advanced weapon states from assisting regional powers to develop weapons of mass destruction; and regional nuclear inspection arrangements, for example, between Argentina and Brazil, India and Pakistan, and, perhaps eventually, the two Koreas. See Leonard S. Spector and Virginia Foran, *Preventing Weapons Proliferation: Should Regimes Be Combined?* Report of 32nd Strategy for Peace, U.S. Foreign Policy Conference (Warrenton, VA: Stanley Foundation, October 1992), pp. 5–6.

30. Off the record briefing by former U.N. peacekeeping official, Detroit, 1993.

31. Thomas Ohlson, ed., *Arms Transfer Limitations and Third World Security* (Oxford: Oxford University Press/SIPRI, 1988), Introduction.

32. Calvin Sims, "For Weapons Makers, a Time to Deal," *New York Times*, January 17, 1993.

33. Ohlson, op. cit., pp. 5–7.

34. Frederic S. Pearson, "Problems and Prospects of Arms Transfer Limitations Among Second-Tier Suppliers: The Cases of France, the United Kingdom and the Federal Republic of Germany," in Ohlson, ibid., p. 127.

35. See Ohlson, ibid., p. 244.

36. See Mark Sommer, "Internationalize Rising World Defense Costs," *Christian Science Monitor,* March 11, 1993.

37. On the uselessness of much modern weaponry, see Mary Kaldor, *The Baroque Arsenal* (New York: Hill and Wang, 1981).

38. Jacques Fontanel and Jean-Francois Guilhaudis, "Arms Transfer Control and Proposals to Link Disarmament to Development," in Ohlson, op. cit., Paper 13. See also Robert S. McNamara, "A Vision of a 'New World Security Order'" (South Bend, IN: Joan B. Kroc Institute for International Peace Studies, Notre Dame University, Fall 1992).

39. Pearson, "Problems and Prospects," p. 145.

40. Michael Klare, "Deadly Convergence: The Arms Trade, Nuclear/Chemical/Missile Proliferation, and Regional Conflict in the 1990s," in *World Security,* pp. 190–193.

41. Anderson, op. cit.

42. Ibid., pp. 778–805.

CHAPTER FIVE

1. The age-old tendency for excess arms to find their way from war to war is continuing. For a general discussion of continuities and discontinuities, see Marek Thee, "Armaments and Disarmament in the Post–Cold War Period: The Quest for a Demilitarized and Nuclear Free World" (Oslo: Norwegian Institute of Human Rights, November 1992, manuscript).

2. John Steinbrunner, remarks to Detroit Committee on Foreign Relations, September 14, 1993.

3. Thee, op. cit., p. 11.

4. Matthew L. Wald, "Nuclear Era Is Departing by Same Door It Entered," *New York Times,* October 31, 1993.

5. Federation of American Scientists, *Arms Sales Monitor,* no. 18 (January 1993): 2. See also Steinbrunner, op. cit.

6. Robert Holzer and Vago Muradian, "Budget Pinch Clouds Future of Exotic Arsenal," *Defense News,* January 18–24, 1993, p. 8.

7. Despite the future possibility of renewed cold war tension, whereas the Red Army ordered some twenty-eight hundred new tanks in 1988 (from a production run of thirty-two hundred, with four hundred going to export), in 1992 Moscow only ordered twenty tanks. See Herbert Wulf, "Arms Industry Limited: The Turning-Point in the 1990s," in *Arms Industry Limited,* ed. Herbert Wulf (Oxford: Oxford University Press, 1993), p. 7.

8. Thee, op. cit., p. 17.

9. Ibid., p. 12.

10. Note, however, that equipment produced for the military has tended to be much more costly, both because of relatively exacting design specifications, or

"milspecs," and because of the larger numbers of personnel assigned to check up on production processes than in the civilian sector.

11. In case such a strategy proved workable, for instance, in the 1993 foreign aid bill Congress provided funding authority for the president to ship up to $50 million in defense equipment to Bosnia from U.S. stocks if the U.N. embargo were lifted and if the president certified that the transfer "would assist that nation in self-defense and thereby promote the security and stability of the region." Federation of American Scientists, *Arms Sales Monitor*, no. 18 (January 1993): 2.

12. Daniel Sneider, "Russia Denies Report of Arms Sales to Serbs," *Christian Science Monitor*, March 2, 1993.

13. Quoted in Edward J. Laurance, *The International Arms Trade* (New York: Lexington, 1992), p. 190.

14. Ibid.

15. Ibid., p. 199.

16. Ibid., p. 201.

17. Andrew Ross, "Dimensions of Militarization in the Third World," *Armed Forces and Society* 13 (Summer 1987): 278.

18. See Michael Barnett and Alexander Wendt, "The Systemic Sources of Dependent Militarization," in *The Insecurity Dilemma: National Security of Third World States*, ed. Brian L. Job (Boulder: Lynne Rienner, 1992), p. 114.

19. Keith Krause, "The Political Economy of the International Arms Transfer System: The Diffusion of Military Technique via Arms Transfers," *International Journal* 45 (Summer 1990): 689–701.

20. Laurance, op. cit., p. 195.

21. Ibid., p. 198.

22. *Defense News*, November 22–28, 1993.

23. Lee Feinstein, "Arms R US," *Bulletin of the Atomic Scientists* 48 (November 1992): 8.

24. See David G. Anderson, "The International Arms Trade: Regulating Conventional Arms Transfers in the Aftermath of the Gulf War," *American University Journal of International Law and Policy* 7 (Summer 1992): 756.

□ □ □

Suggested Readings

ARMAMENTS: HISTORY AND DEVELOPMENT

Cordesman, Anthony H., and Abraham R. Wagner. *The Lessons of Modern War.* 3 Vols. Boulder: Westview, 1990.

Dyson, Freeman. *Disturbing the Universe.* New York: Harper and Row, 1979.

_____. *Weapons and Hope.* New York: Harper and Row, 1984.

Gleditsch, Nils Petter, and Olav Njolstad. *Arms Races: Technological and Political Dynamics.* London: Sage/Peace Research Institute, Oslo, 1990.

Katz, James E., ed. *Sowing the Dragon's Teeth: The Implications of Third World Military Industrialization.* Lexington, MA: Lexington Books, 1986.

Krause, Keith. *Arms and the State: Patterns of Military Production and Trade.* Cambridge: Cambridge University Press, 1992.

Neuman, Stephanie G., and Robert E. Harkavy. *The Lessons of Recent Wars in the Third World.* Volume II. Lexington, MA: Lexington Books, 1987.

Norman, Colin. *The God That Limps: Science and Technology in the Eighties.* New York: Norton, 1981.

O'Connell, Robert L. *Of Arms and Men: A History of War, Weapons, and Aggression.* Oxford: Oxford University Press, 1989.

Van Creveld, Martin. *Technology and War: From 2000 B.C. to the Present.* New York: Free Press, 1989.

ARMAMENTS AND ARMS TRANSFERS: INDUSTRY AND GOVERNMENT POLICY

Anthony, Ian, ed. *Arms Trade and the Medium Powers.* Brighton, UK: Harvester, Wheatsheaf, 1992.

Brogan, Patrick. *Deadly Business: Sam Cummings, Interarms, and the Arms Trade.* New York: Norton, 1983.

Brzoska, Michael, and Thomas Ohlson. *Arms Transfers to the Third World, 1971–1985.* Oxford: Oxford University Press/SIPRI, 1987.

Brzoska, Michael, and Thomas Ohlson, eds. *Arms Production in the Third World.* London: Taylor and Francis, 1986.

Ferrari, Paul L., Jeffrey W. Knopf, and Raul L. Madrid. *U.S. Arms Exports: Policies and Contractors.* Washington, DC: Investor Responsibility Research Center, 1987.

135

Gansler, Jacques S. *The Defense Industry.* Cambridge: MIT Press, 1988.

George, Alexander. *Forceful Persuasion: Coercive Diplomacy as an Alternative to War.* Washington, DC: U.S. Institute of Peace Press, 1991.

Kapstein, Ethan Barnaby. *The Political Economy of National Security: A Global Perspective.* New York: McGraw-Hill, 1992.

Kolodziej, Edward A. *Making and Marketing Arms: The French Experience and Its Implications for the International System.* Princeton: Princeton University Press, 1987.

Laurance, Edward J. *The International Arms Trade.* New York: Lexington, 1992.

Nachmias, Nitza. *Transfer of Arms, Leverage, and Peace in the Middle East.* New York: Greenwood Press, 1988.

Neuman, Stephanie. *Military Assistance in Recent Wars.* Washington Papers, no. 122. New York: Praeger, 1986.

Payne, James L. *Why Nations Arm.* Oxford: Basil Blackwell, 1989.

Sanders, Ralph. *Arms Industries: New Suppliers and Regional Security.* Washington: National Defense University Press, 1990.

Wulf, Herbert, ed. *Arms Industry Limited.* Oxford: Oxford University Press, 1993.

ARMAMENT: MASS DESTRUCTION

Schroeer, Dietrich. *Science, Technology, and the Nuclear Arms Race.* New York: Wiley, 1984.

Smoke, Richard. *National Security and the Nuclear Dilemma: An Introduction to the American Experience.* 3d ed. New York: McGraw-Hill, 1993.

Spector, Leonard S., with Jacqueline R. Smith. *Nuclear Ambitions: The Spread of Nuclear Weapons, 1989–1990.* Boulder: Westview, 1990.

ARMAMENT: GENERAL SOURCES AND PERIODICALS

Bulletin of the Atomic Scientists.

Defense News.

Federation of American Scientists. *Arms Trade Monitor.*

Grimmett, Richard F. *Trends in Conventional Arms Transfers to the Third World.* Washington, DC: Congressional Research Service.

International Institute for Strategic Studies. Annually. *The Military Balance.* London.

Jane's Defence Weekly.

Stockholm International Peace Research Institute (SIPRI). *Yearbooks.*

SIPRI. *The Arms Trade with the Third World.* Stockholm: Almqvist and Wicksell, 1971.

Sivard, Ruth Leger. Annually. *World Military and Social Expenditures.* Washington, DC: World Priorities.

U.S. Arms Control and Disarmament Agency. Annually. *World Military Expenditures and Arms Transfers.* Washington, DC.

ARMS CONTROL AND REGULATION

Anthony, Ian, ed. *Arms Export Regulations*. London: Oxford University Press, 1991.

Bellany, Ian. *A Basis for Arms Control*. Aldershot, UK: Dartmouth, 1991.

Carnesale, Albert, and Richard N. Haass, eds. *Superpower Arms Control: Setting the Record Straight*. Cambridge, MA: Ballinger, 1987.

Goldman, Ralph M. *Arms Control and Peacekeeping*. New York: Random House, 1982.

Jensen, Lloyd. *Negotiating Nuclear Arms Control*. Columbia: University of South Carolina Press, 1988.

Klare, Michael T., and Daniel C. Thomas, eds. *World Security: Trends and Challenges at Century's End*. New York: St. Martin's, 1991.

Laurance, Edward J., Siemon T. Wezeman, and Herbert Wulf. *Arms Watch: SIPRI Report on the First Year of the UN Register of Conventional Arms*. Oxford: Oxford University Press, 1993.

Ohlson, Thomas, ed. *Arms Transfer Limitations and Third World Security*. Oxford: Oxford University Press/SIPRI, 1988.

Rogers, Paul, and Malcolm Dando. *A Violent Peace: Global Security After the Cold War*. London: Brassey's, 1992.

□ □ □

Glossary

An **antiballistic missile** is capable of knocking down another missile in flight. Its development was severely restricted by a treaty between the United States and the USSR in 1972.

Areas-of-crisis regulations are export prohibitions adopted by some arms-supplying states, such as Germany and Sweden, attempting to keep their arms from further inflaming war-prone regions.

Arms control is the agreement or process used to limit the development, deployment, or use of various types of weapons—with limits on the quantity or quality (or both) of the weapons involved.

An **arms transfer** is the dispatch of weapons or related materials from one country to another by sale, loan, or gift. Agreements can be between governments, private parties, or both.

Attrition is the wear and tear and resultant breakdown as well as the destruction of equipment in battle.

The **Boxer Rebellion** was an attack in 1900 on foreigners and Chinese Christians by young militant Chinese rebels belonging to a secret society, the Fists of Righteous Harmony. The Boxers considered themselves impervious to foreign weapons, but a seven-nation coalition broke the rebellion and imposed crushing financial penalties on the crumbling Manchu dynasty.

A **buyer's market** refers to the situation where the market supply exceeds general demand so that sellers are at a disadvantage relative to a buyer's options to shop around.

Collateral damage occurs when explosive devices aimed at a target injure or kill people or destroy other property nearby.

Comparative advantage is the most efficiently produced or reasonably priced export items a country can offer.

Conditionality comprises provisions that require certain policies in exchange for agreement to provide financial or military assistance, such as requirements to reduce defense spending.

Confidence building is reassurance to an enemy and attempts to build trust through means such as giving advance notice of military moves or exercises and allowing observation thereof.

Consortia are groups of companies or units acting together on specific projects.

Continental defense is the strategy of defending the homeland close to its own borders rather than deploying military forces at great distances.

The **Conventional Forces in Europe (CFE) Agreement** is a U.S.-Soviet agreement of the late 1980s to slash the number of conventional land-based weapons faced off across Eastern and Western Europe and either destroy or withdraw them from those zones.

Cost-plus contracts are government contracts with weapons manufacturers that allow extra payments for unforeseen production problems.

Countertrade refers to measures demanded by today's arms buyers to obtain compensation for the high cost of weapons; such measures entail agreement by the arms seller to purchase a certain amount of the buyer's products in return.

Defense conversion is the process of switching from defense to nondefense production or land use (e.g., decommissioning military bases).

Deterrence means measures to dissuade or prevent an opponent from taking some action.

Disarmament is the giving up or destroying of a nation's arms.

Diversification is the process by which governments find alternate sources for arms or companies develop alternate products rather than relying solely on one product line.

Dual use refers to equipment designed to be used in either military or civilian products.

Economies of scale are the benefits in reduced cost per unit derived by larger enterprises and longer production runs from such effects as manufacturers being able to purchase larger quantities of raw materials at lower prices.

End use statements are stated expectations in arms export licenses about the final destination and uses allowed for the weapons.

Forward defense is the strategy of meeting foreign threats at a distance from a state's own borders rather than waiting for an attack on the homeland.

Horizontal proliferation is the spread of weapons to more and more countries.

Indigenous means produced or originated inside a given country.

Industrial policy comprises government moves to set targets and goals or offer subsidies for developing and nurturing certain types of industries.

An **intergovernmental organization (IGO)** is an international organization whose members are nation-states.

The **Intermediate Nuclear Forces Agreement** is a 1988 U.S.-Soviet agreement to eliminate land-based, medium-range (300–3,400 miles), nuclear weapon missile delivery systems in Europe and Asia.

The **International Atomic Energy Agency (IAEA)** is an intergovernmental organization formed under U.N. auspices in the 1950s that became responsible for tracking weapons-grade nuclear fuels and inspecting production facilities under the NPT of 1970.

The **international power structure** is the hierarchy or rank-ordering of countries in the world, or in a region, by factors such as military power, technological advancement, or economic output.

A **learning curve** is the increased production efficiency that results from greater experience and more output.

Less developed countries (LDCs) are traditional countries with restricted industrial capacity (often referred to as the Third World).

Militarism is the tendency for military values to permeate a society.

Militarized describes a situation or policy that takes on military characteristics, including the use of force.

The **military-industrial complex** is the coincidence of interests between industrialists and military officials.

The **Missile Technology Control Regime (MTCR)** is a 1987 agreement among the most advanced missile-producing countries to limit the distribution of nuclear-capable ballistic missiles and relevant technology among other states.

Multilateral means involving more than two countries cooperatively.

A **multiple independently targeted reenty vehicle (MIRV)** is a self-guiding missile nose cone containing several separately targeted nuclear bombs.

Mutual assured destruction, sometimes known as MAD, was a policy of nuclear deterrence between the United States and the USSR in which each deployed nuclear weapons in such a way as to assure the weapons could guarantee a massive retaliation by whichever side was attacked first. Hence, first attacks would be discouraged.

A **neutron bomb** is an enhanced radiation nuclear weapon, developed during the 1970s and 1980s, to threaten greater radiation concentration against troops and personnel and less blast damage to surrounding towns.

A **newly industrializing country (NIC)** was an LDC that has scored significant economic progress in new industries.

A **nuclear-free zone** is an area or region where states have agreed to prevent the establishment of nuclear arsenals either by supplying or receiving the weapons.

The **nuclear-freeze campaign** was a U.S. movement during the 1980s to halt nuclear weapon production and modernization.

The **Nuclear Non-proliferation Treaty (NPT)** is an agreement, which entered into force in 1970 and now has more than 140 states as signatories, not to give or acquire nuclear weapons in return for nuclear arms reductions among major powers and minor power access to peaceful nuclear technology.

The **Nuclear Suppliers Group** is an informal consultative arrangement among states that export weapons-grade nuclear fuels.

Arms trade **offsets** are measures taken by arms suppliers to compensate arms buyers for the high cost of weapons; such measures can include agreement to provide technical advice and technology to help the buyer establish new industries of its own.

On-site inspection refers to checking on compliance with arms control agreements by observers at weapons storage or deployment sites.

Overkill refers to excessive, and particularly nuclear, destructive capability above that theoretically necessary to deter or defeat an enemy.

A **peace dividend** is the expected gains to be made in lowered defense budgets at times of peace or reduced tensions.

Proliferation is the spread of weapons.

Reexport refers to the export of arms that were originally obtained by import.

Regimes are agreements or the joint development of organizations among countries to regulate international behavior or outcomes.

Restructuring comprises actions taken by firms to become more competitive, such as mergers, acquisitions, joint production or marketing (often across national boundaries), the finding of new products, the reorganization of management, and the cutting of costs (often by reducing work forces).

Retrofitting means adapting parts from one weapon system to modify or improve another.

Standard operating procedures (SOPS) are bureaucratic routines for accomplishing tasks.

Strategic means involving major security threats or interests.

The **Strategic Defense Initiative** was a U.S. attempt during the 1980s to build a space-based antinuclear defense system.

Strategic materials are natural resources that are of great importance to defense and military production.

Transnational actors are participants in world politics that operate across national boundaries and do not necessarily owe allegiance to any one country; these can include intergovernmental or nongovernmental organizations, terrorists, and multinational business enterprises.

Transparency refers to procedures to report agreements to transfer weapons and weapons deliveries to international accounting agencies.

Verification refers to procedures to check on compliance with arms control and disarmament agreements.

Vertical proliferation is the transfer and spread of higher levels of weapons technology in the international system.

Warheads are nuclear bombs in missile nose cones.

□ □ □

About the Book
and Author

Today, despite the end of the cold war, more countries have more sophisticated weapons from more numerous suppliers than ever before. This is partly a product of continuing and growing conflicts—especially regional and interethnic ones—but it also reflects the political and economic difficulties of weaning public and private enterprise away from powerful and highly lucrative defense manufacturing and sales.

In this compact yet comprehensive volume, Frederic Pearson surveys the broad terrain covered by the concept of "the security dilemma" and points out landmarks along the route proceeding from proliferation to economic interests, to potential "conversion," to the future of defense production and marketing. Along the way we experience the lure of arms sales expositions and fairs and the quandary of deciding whether to arm victims of aggression. The author meticulously describes and documents the twin motives of "welfare and security" in the arms market: who buys weapons, who sells them, where they are produced, and how they are—and are not—used. Through a combination of data, anecdotes, illustrations, and narration accompanied by special feature boxes, we see how arms races have mounted historically and how they might be defused in this, the gathering post–cold war order.

From spears and axes to the radar-eluding stealth aircraft, *The Global Spread of Arms* charts the history of the arms dilemma and brings us up-to-date on myths and recent trends in weapons development internationally. Touching on issues ranging from multinational arms manufacturers to black and gray market consumers, from arms verification to arms autonomy, and from peace dividends to "peace through strength," Pearson presents a balanced view of the policy debate about defense economies, collective security, and how to manage them.

Governments of developed and developing countries alike talk about arms control but often fail to act in curtailing arms trade and transfers. Nowhere is the paradox of the "sovereign right to arm" more apparent than in current hot spots detailed by Pearson, including the Balkans, the former Soviet Union, Iraq, North Korea, and South Asia. We see an array of arms trends played out to devastating effect: sanctions, embargoes, multilateral trade and negotiations, smuggling, "arms balancing," and, ultimately, proliferation and escalation cycles. Potential escape routes from weapons dilemmas also are offered in a full review of arms transfer controls.

Students of international relations and international political economy, from peace studies to security studies, will join industry and government professionals as well as general readers in finding this primer indispensable to understanding the past and future global arsenal.

Frederic S. Pearson is director of the Center for Peace and Conflict Studies and professor of political science at Wayne State University.

BOOKS IN THIS SERIES

Deborah J. Gerner
**One Land, Two Peoples:
The Conflict over Palestine**

☐ ☐ ☐

Kenneth W. Grundy
**South Africa: Domestic Crisis
and Global Challenge**

☐ ☐ ☐

Gareth Porter and Janet Welsh Brown
Global Environmental Politics

☐ ☐ ☐

Davis S. Mason
**Revolution in East-Central Europe
and World Politics**

☐ ☐ ☐

Georg Sørensen
**Democracy and Democratization:
Processes and Prospects in a Changing World**

☐ ☐ ☐

Steve Chan
**East Asian Dynamism: Growth, Order, and
Security in the Pacific Region, second edition**

☐ ☐ ☐

Barry B. Hughes
**International Futures: Choices in
the Creation of a New World Order**

☐ ☐ ☐

Jack Donnelly
International Human Rights

☐ ☐ ☐

V. Spike Peterson and Anne Sisson Runyan
Global Gender Issues

☐ ☐ ☐

Sarah J. Tisch and Michael B. Wallace
**Dilemmas of Development Assistance:
The What, Why, and Who of Foreign Aid**

Index